MARKETING
4.0

"The technology world moves so quickly today that each change accelerates the next. It's critical in such an environment to have a baseline and point of reference to help marketers find their way forward. *Marketing 4.0* puts a new scholarship stake in the ground and will be the starting point and an invaluable resource for everyone trying to invent and understand the digital and mobile future."

—**Howard Tullman**, CEO,
Chicagoland Entrepreneurial Center/1871

"The Internet and IT radically change marketing. This book is the eye-opener for marketing in the new era."

—**Hermann Simon**, Founder and Chairman,
Simon-Kucher & Partners

"No one has a finger on the pulse of marketing like Phil Kotler. His ability to identify and interpret new marketing trends and developments is truly astounding. Once again, with *Marketing 4.0*, Kotler and his co-authors help to blaze a new trail to marketing success. This is definitely the one marketing book you HAVE to read this year."

—**Kevin Lane Keller**, E.B. Osborn
Professor of Marketing, Tuck School of Business

"Kotler and his associates have beautifully synthesized today's digital, interactive marketplace and marketing's new role."

—**Don Schultz**, Professor (Emeritus-in-Service) of Integrated
Marketing Communications, Medill School at Northwestern University

"No one is more qualified than Philip Kotler, the father of marketing, to document the enormous changes taking place in the field today. The future of marketing is digital and this book is your guide."

—**Al Ries**, Author of
Positioning: The Battle for Your Mind

"As the world of marketing increasingly grapples with digital transformation, *Marketing 4.0* offers an exciting framework along with examples for practitioners."

—**Nirmalya Kumar**, Professor of Marketing,
London Business School

"A terrific guide to the transformations that are already coming over the horizon to challenge marketing practice. Perplexed marketers will learn how to navigate the power shifts and possibilities of digital connectivity and turn them into advantages."
—**George S. Day**, Geoffrey T. Boisi Professor Emeritus,
Wharton School of the University of Pennsylvania

"I am often overwhelmed by the variety and the speed of change, in spite of being in marketing consulting for forty years. I am therefore happy that the 'guru' Philip Kotler, who began with *Marketing 1.0* over four decades ago, is still with us to make another significant contribution with *Marketing 4.0*—guidelines to deal with changes today, especially those brought about by the IT revolution and changing consumer profiles."

—**Walter Vieira**, Marketing Consultant, Author,
Visiting Professor, Past Chairman of
International Council of Management Consulting Institutes

MARKETING 4.0

4.0

Moving

from Traditional

to Digital

PHILIP KOTLER

HERMAWAN KARTAJAYA

IWAN SETIAWAN

WILEY

To the next generation of marketers and behavioral economists, who will enhance the economic, social, and environmental contributions that marketing makes to the welfare of people and the planet

—Philip Kotler

*To President Joko Widodo, Marketeer of the Year Indonesia–Government 2010-2012 and A New Hope (*Time *magazine, October 27, 2014)*

—Hermawan Kartajaya

To my family and friends and everyone else around me who has become my f-factor and made me a better human

—Iwan Setiawan

CONTENTS

ix

ACKNOWLEDGMENTS

Marketing 4.0 was six years in the making. Over this period, a number of people have contributed to the completion of the book. The authors would like to thank the WOW team at MarkPlus, Inc., who conducted the research and spent countless hours brainstorming with the authors: Yosanova Savitry, Vendy Chandra, Cecilia Hermanto, Kevin Leonard, Quincy Wongso, Edwin Hardi, Adrian Hudiono, Evita Tania, Shabrina Annisarasyiq, Andre Anggada, and Fachriza Prathama.

We would also like to thank the leaders at MarkPlus, Inc.—The Council—who have invested their thoughts and energy in the book: Michael Hermawan, Jacky Mussry, Taufik, Hendra Warsita, Vivie Jericho, Stephanie Hermawan, and Ence.

Last but not least, we would like to thank the team at Wiley—Richard Narramore, Tiffany Colon, and Jocelyn Kwiatkowski—who made it possible for us to share *Marketing 3.0* and *Marketing 4.0* with the world.

PROLOGUE

FROM *MARKETING 3.0* TO *MARKETING 4.0*

For the past six years, marketers whom we met around the world have been asking for a sequel to *Marketing 3.0*. Considering the dynamics of marketing, many would expect *Marketing 4.0* to be in the pipeline.

In *Marketing 3.0*, we talked about the major shift from product-driven marketing (1.0) to customer-centric marketing (2.0), and ultimately to human-centric marketing (3.0). In *Marketing 3.0*, we observed customers transforming into whole human beings with minds, hearts, and spirits. Therefore, we argued that the future of marketing lies in creating products, services, and company cultures that embrace and reflect human values. Since the book was published in 2010, many marketers have been adopting the principles of *Marketing 3.0*. The book was so universally accepted that it has been translated into 24 languages besides English globally.

A year after the book was published, we built the Museum of Marketing 3.0 in Ubud, Bali. The museum was built with the kind support of the three princes of Ubud: Tjokorda Gde Putra Sukawati, Tjokorda Gde Oka Sukawati, and Tjokorda Gde Raka Sukawati. Ubud, with its aura of spirituality, is indeed the perfect place for the first marketing museum of its kind. In the museum, we have been curating inspiring cases of marketers, companies, and marketing campaigns that embrace the human spirit. The contents are organized in a modern multiscreen setup. In recent years, the museum has been upgraded with advanced technologies such as augmented reality and virtual reality.

Indeed, a lot has happened since we wrote *Marketing 3.0*, especially in terms of technological advancements. The technologies we are seeing today are not new. But they have been converging in recent years, and the collective impact of that convergence has greatly affected marketing practices around the world. New trends are emerging from this: the "sharing" economy, the "now" economy, omnichannel integration, content marketing, social CRM, and many other things.

We believe that the technology convergence will ultimately lead to the convergence between digital marketing and traditional marketing. In a high-tech world, people long for high touch. The more social we are, the more we want things that are made just for us. Backed by big-data analytics, products become more personalized and services become more personal. In the digital economy, the key is to leverage these paradoxes.

In this transitional era, a new marketing approach is required. Thus, we introduce *Marketing 4.0* as the natural outgrowth of *Marketing 3.0*. The major premise of this book is that marketing should adapt to the changing nature of customer paths in the digital economy. The role of marketers is to guide customers throughout their journey from awareness and ultimately to advocacy.

The first part of the book is the result of our observation of the world we are living in. We start by embracing the three power shifts that are shaping our world. We move further by exploring how connectivity has fundamentally changed human lives. Moreover, we take a deeper look into the major digital subcultures of youth, women, and netizens that will serve as foundations for a completely new breed of customer.

The second and core part of the book discusses how marketers can boost productivity by understanding customer paths in the digital era. It introduces a new set of marketing metrics and a whole new way of looking at our marketing practices. We will also dive deep into several key industries and learn how to implement the ideas of *Marketing 4.0* in those industries.

Finally, the third part describes in detail the major tactics of *Marketing 4.0*. We start with human-centric marketing, which aims to humanize brands with humanlike attributes. We then explore content marketing in greater detail in order to create customer conversations. Moreover, we also describe how marketers can implement omnichannel marketing for higher sales. Finally, we dig into the concept of customer engagement in the digital era.

In essence, *Marketing 4.0* describes a deepening and a broadening of human-centric marketing to cover every aspect of the customer's journey. We are hopeful that you will find insights and inspirations from this book and join us in redefining marketing in the years to come.

ABOUT THE AUTHORS

Philip Kotler, the S.C. Johnson & Son Distinguished Professor of International Marketing at the Kellogg School of Management, Northwestern University, is widely regarded as the Father of Modern Marketing. He is ranked by the *Wall Street Journal* as one of the top six most influential business thinkers. The recipient of numerous awards and honorary degrees from schools all over the world, he holds an MA from the University of Chicago and a PhD from the Massachusetts Institute of Technology (MIT), both in economics. Philip has an incredible international presence—his books have been translated into approximately 25 languages, and he regularly speaks on the international circuit.

Hermawan Kartajaya is the founder and Executive Chairman of MarkPlus, Inc., and is one of the "50 Gurus Who Have Shaped the Future of Marketing," according to the Chartered Institute of Marketing, United Kingdom. Hermawan is also a recipient of the Distinguished Global Leadership Award from Pan-Pacific Business Association at the University of Nebraska-Lincoln. He is the current President of the Asia Council for Small Business—a regional council of affiliates and chapters of the International Council for Small Business—and a co-founder of the Asia Marketing Federation.

Iwan Setiawan serves as the Chief Operating Officer of MarkPlus, Inc. (www.markplusinc.com), where he helps businesses design their marketing strategies. A frequent writer and speaker, Iwan is also the Editor-in-Chief of Marketeers (www.marketeers.com). Iwan holds an MBA from the Kellogg School of Management at Northwestern University and a BEng from the University of Indonesia.

Part I
Fundamental Trends Shaping Marketing

1 Power Shifts to the Connected Customers

From Vertical, Exclusive, and Individual to Horizontal, Inclusive, and Social

Charlie Frost was a conspiracy theorist who strongly believed that 2012 would bring the end of civilization. A couple of geologists in 2009 found that Frost's belief might be true. They discovered that the earth's core was about to explode and bring catastrophe to the world. And so the world's leaders gathered to find a solution and decided to build giant ships resembling Noah's Ark to save select groups of the world's population. The survivors on the ships would be expected to start a new civilization.

This story is completely fictional and is taken from the movie *2012*. But many of the scenes in the movie symbolize the change we are experiencing today. The movie shows how the old standards of civilization—political, economic, socio-cultural, and religious standards—were being destroyed and being replaced by a more horizontal and inclusive set of social standards. It shows how leaders of the Western superpower countries were forced to drop their egos and collaborate. They even had to rely on China to build the giant ships. The ships also functioned as the symbols of a new world in which diverse people were connected with one another without any geographical and demographical boundaries.

Today, we are living in a whole new world. The power structure we have come to know is experiencing drastic changes. The internet, which brought connectivity and transparency to our lives, has been largely responsible for these power shifts.

We witness how exclusive powers surrender to the power of inclusivity. The G7, which is an exclusive group of powerful nations, could not solve the global financial crisis by themselves. They had to involve the G20 nations, which include China, India, and Indonesia. The economic power is now more inclusively dispersed. Large corporations also found it difficult to nurture innovation within their exclusive organizations. Companies such as Microsoft and Amazon eventually needed to acquire smaller yet more innovative companies such as Skype and Zappos. Even millionaires Bill Gates and Mark Zuckerberg were aware of the need for economic inclusivity. They donated their wealth to help the poor through the Bill and Melinda Gates Foundation and the Startup:Education (now part of the Chan Zuckerberg Initiative) organizations, respectively.

We are also seeing how a vertical power structure has been diluted by a more horizontal force. Take, for example, how at the top of the world's most populous countries is the "United States of Facebook" with its population of 1.65 billion people. We also see how people now go to Twitter for breaking news from citizen journalists whereas in the past, a large TV network like CNN would be the go-to channel. Even YouTube has taken Hollywood by storm. A survey commissioned by *Variety* magazine revealed that for 13- to 18-year-olds, YouTube celebrities are more popular than Hollywood stars. The entertainment giant Sony collaborated with YouTube to show that horizontal forces could not be hindered by vertical ones. Sony's North Korea–themed comedy movie *The Interview* was commercially released first via YouTube in response to an alleged cyberattack from North Korea.

The power shift also influences people. Now, the power lies not with individuals but with social groups. Dictators were overthrown by people led by unknown leaders. Wall Street financiers were shaken by the Occupy Wall Street protest movement. Ebola fighters were chosen as *Time* magazine's 2014 Person of the Year rather than U.S. President Barack Obama or Indian Prime Minister Narendra Modi.

These shifts have radically changed our world. In a world where the horizontal, inclusive, and social forces trump the vertical, exclusive, and individual forces, customer communities have become ever more powerful. They are now more vocal. They are not afraid of big companies and big brands. They love to share stories, good and bad, about brands.

Random conversations about brands are now more credible than targeted advertising campaigns. Social circles have become the main source of influence, overtaking external marketing communications and even personal preference. Customers tend to follow the lead of their peers when deciding which brand to choose. It is as if customers were protecting themselves from false brand claims and campaign trickeries by using their social circles to build a fortress.

From Exclusive to Inclusive

Gone are the days when being exclusive was the goal. Inclusivity has become the new name of the game. At the macro level, the world is moving from a hegemony to a multilateral power structure. The superpowers, mainly the European Union and the United States, realize that some economic powers are shifting to the rest of the world, most notably to Asia, which has experienced steady growth in recent years. It is important to note that the Western superpowers will still be powerful; it's just that other nations are gaining more power over time. Economic powers are no longer concentrated but are more evenly distributed.

This economic shift is often attributed to the demographic profile of the emerging market populations: younger, more productive, and growing in terms of income level. It has created strong demand for products and services, which in turn drives economic growth. Recent data, however, suggest that the reason might not just be demographic.

From the innovation perspective, emerging markets are also heading in a better direction. Recent data collected by Robert Litan suggests that innovation in the United States has been declining. The number of start-ups accounted for only 8 percent of total companies in the country, whereas 30 years ago, it was nearly 15 percent. In Litan's data, the number of bankruptcies exceeded the number of start-ups.

The trajectory for Asia is quite the opposite. According to the Organization for Economic Cooperation and Development, China will overtake the European Union and the United States in innovation-related spending by 2019. In 2012, South Korea became the most advanced country for innovation, spending over 4 percent of its GDP on research and development.

The political influence of the Western world is also declining, following the drop in its economic influence. Military powers that used to provide effective influence are slowly being replaced by the soft approach of economic support and diplomacy. China, for example, maintains a strong influence in Africa due to its support for developing better governance and a more sustainable development.

Business itself is moving toward inclusivity. Technology enables both automation and miniaturization, which bring down product costs and allow companies to serve the new emerging markets. The disruptive innovations across business sectors have brought cheaper and simpler products to the poor, formerly considered a "non-market." Products and services once considered exclusive are now available to mass markets all over the world. Examples include Tata Nano's $2,000 car and Aravind Eye Care System's $16 cataract surgery.

This also works the other way around. With reverse innovation, new products can be developed and introduced in the emerging markets before being sold elsewhere. The frugality and cost-consciousness shown in developing products are becoming the new sources of differentiation. A well-known example of this is GE's Mac 400, a portable battery-operated electrocardiogram machine, which was designed to serve rural villagers in India. It was marketed elsewhere with portability as its core differentiation.

The transparency brought by the internet also enables entrepreneurs from emerging countries to draw inspiration from their counterparts in developed countries. They are building clone businesses marked by local twists in the execution. There are, for example,

Amazon-inspired Flipkart.com from India, Groupon-inspired Disdus from Indonesia, PayPal-inspired Alipay in China, and Uber-inspired Grab in Malaysia. Customers in these countries experience the services without having to wait for American companies to establish their footprints there.

The walls between industries are also blurring. The convergence and integration of two or more industries are trending. Industries have the choice to either compete or synergize to reach the same customers. In most cases, they synergize.

Many medical centers are now integrated with tourism facilities so that the costs of health care and holiday can be optimized. United Kingdom–based Patients Beyond Borders estimated serving around 11 million medical tourists in 2013. Popular medical treatments and destinations include dental work in Costa Rica, heart operations in Malaysia, and cosmetic surgery in Brazil.

In some emerging markets where prepaid cellular phone usage is immense, the telecommunications sector is collaborating with financial services to provide payment channels for goods and services. A well-known example is the M-Pesa, a mobile-based money transfer firm in Kenya.

Within an established industry, the sub-sectors will also be difficult to distinguish. In the financial-services industry, the lines that now separate banking, financing, insurance, fund management, and other industry sub-sectors will fade away, making it imperative for financial institutions to find new ways to differentiate themselves. Vertical integration in one industry will create business entities that engage in comprehensive roles from material supply to production to distribution, making it difficult to define in which business a company is active.

At a more micro level, humans are embracing social inclusivity. Being inclusive is not about being similar; it is about living harmoniously despite differences. In the online world, social media has redefined the way people interact with one another, enabling people to build relationships without geographic and demographic barriers. The impact of social media does not stop there. It also facilitates global collaborations in innovation. Consider Wikipedia, which was built by a countless number of people, or InnoCentive, which broadcasts research and development challenges and asks for the best solutions. In fact, all social media that take a crowd-sourcing approach are good examples of social inclusivity. Social media drives social inclusivity and gives people the sense of belonging to their communities.

Social inclusivity is happening not only online but offline as well. The concept of *inclusive cities*—cities that welcome the diversity of their inhabitants—are often dubbed as a good model for sustainable cities. Similar to the concept of social media, the concept of inclusive cities argues that when cities welcome minorities who are often left behind and give them a sense of acceptance, that will only benefit the cities. Social inclusivity can also appear in the form of fair trade, employment diversity, and empowerment of women. These practices embrace human differences across gender, race, and economic status. Brands like the Body Shop are building a strong commitment to social inclusivity with values such as "support community trade" and programs such as "stop violence in the home."

From Vertical to Horizontal

Globalization creates a level playing field. The competitiveness of companies will no longer be determined by their size, country of origin, or past advantage. Smaller, younger, and locally based companies will have a chance to compete against bigger, older, and global companies. Eventually, there will be no company that overly dominates the others. Instead, a company can be more competitive if it can connect with communities of customers and partners for co-creation and with competitors for co-opetition.

The flow of innovation that was once vertical (from companies to the market) has become horizontal. In the past, companies believed that innovation should come from within; thus, they built a strong research and development infrastructure. Eventually, they realized that the rate of internal innovation was never fast enough for them to be competitive in the ever-changing market. Procter & Gamble (P&G), for example, learned this early in 2000, when its sales from new products flattened. It later transformed its research-and-develop model into a connect-and-develop model. The more horizontal model relies on outside sources for ideas that in turn will be commercialized using internal P&G capabilities. Its rival Unilever has been moving in the same direction by capitalizing on its vast external innovation ecosystem. Today, innovation is horizontal; the market supplies the ideas, and companies commercialize the ideas.

Similarly, the concept of competition is changing from vertical to horizontal. Technology is the main cause. Chris Anderson's long tail hypothesis could not be truer today. The market is shifting away from high-volume mainstream brands into low-volume niche ones. With the internet, physical logistical constraints no longer exist for smaller companies and brands.

This inclusivity now enables companies to enter industries that they would not otherwise have entered in the past. This provides opportunities for companies to grow but poses significant competitive threats. Because distinctions between industries are blurring, it will be highly challenging for companies to keep track of their competitors. Competitors in the future will come from the same industry as well as from other relevant and connected industries. A few years ago, taxi companies and hotel chains would not imagine competing for passengers and guests with technology start-ups such as Uber and Airbnb, which provide private transportation and lodging. To spot latent competitors, companies should start with the customers' objectives and consider potential alternatives that customers might accept to achieve their objectives.

Companies should also track competitors from outside their home markets. These competitors are not necessarily multinational corporations. In recent years, we have observed the rise of great companies from emerging markets such as Xiaomi and Oppo. These companies innovate out of necessity and were created in challenging home markets. They match the quality of major brands but with significantly lower prices. This is made possible by the online go-to-market option. Highly innovative and resilient, these companies have all the necessary ingredients to expand their markets globally.

The concept of customer trust is no longer vertical; it is now horizontal. Customers in the past were easily influenced by marketing campaigns. They also sought for and listened to authority and expertise. But recent research across industries show that most customers believe more in the f-factor (friends, families, Facebook fans, Twitter followers) than in marketing communications. Most ask strangers on social media for advice and trust them more than they do advertising and expert opinions. In recent years, the trend has spurred the growth of communal rating systems such as TripAdvisor and Yelp.

In such a context, a brand should no longer view customers as mere targets. In the past, it was common for companies to broadcast their message through various advertisement media. Some companies even invented a not-so-authentic differentiation to be able to stand out from the crowd and support their brand image. Consequently, the brand is often treated as outer-shell packaging, which allows for a fake representation of its true value. This approach will no longer be effective because with the help of their communities, customers guard themselves against bad brands that target them.

A relationship between brands and customers should no longer be vertical but instead it should be horizontal. Customers should be considered peers and friends of the brand. The brand should reveal its authentic character and be honest of its true value. Only then will the brand be trustworthy.

From Individual to Social

When making purchase decisions, customers have typically been driven by individual preference as well as by a desire for social conformity. The level of importance for each of these two factors varies from one person to another. It also varies across industries and categories.

Given the connectivity we live in today, the weight of social conformity is increasing across the board. Customers care more and more about the opinions of others. They also share their opinions and compile massive pools of reviews. Together, customers paint their own picture of companies and brands, which is often very different from the image that companies and brands intend to project. The internet, especially social media, has facilitated this major shift by providing the platform and tools.

This trend will continue. Virtually everyone on earth will be connected very soon. It turns out that the solution for the internet laggards was not cheap laptops but rather cheap smartphones. In fact, it is projected by the UMTS Forum that mobile data traffic will jump by a factor of 33 from 2010 to 2020. With such vast connectivity, market behavior will become significantly different. For example, in many countries in-store research using mobile phones to compare prices and check reviews is trending. Mobile connectivity allows customers to access the wisdom of the crowd and to make better purchase decisions.

In such an environment, customers conform more to social opinions. In fact, most personal purchase decisions will essentially be social decisions. Customers communicate with one another and converse about brands and companies. From a marketing communications point of view, customers are no longer passive targets but are becoming active media of communications. A beauty products brand—Sephora —has been exploring communities as a new form of media assets. Sephora has built a social media community in which all community-generated content is incorporated into the Beauty Talk platform. It has become a trusted medium for customers who are trying to consult with other members of the community.

Embracing this trend is not easy. Companies used to have control over marketing communications, and they used to handle customer complaints individually. With community-generated content, companies have no control over the conversation. Censoring content will weaken credibility. They must also be prepared for massive social backlash when something goes wrong.

That being said, companies and brands that have strong reputations and honest claims about their products should have nothing to worry about. But those who make false claims and have poor products will not survive. It is practically impossible to hide flaws or isolate customer complaints in a transparent, digital world.

Summary: Horizontal, Inclusive, and Social

Marketers need to embrace the shift to a more horizontal, inclusive, and social business landscape. The market is becoming more inclusive. Social media eliminate geographic and demographic barriers, enabling people to connect and communicate and companies to innovate through collaboration. Customers are becoming more horizontally oriented. They are becoming increasingly wary of marketing communications from brands and are relying instead on the f-factor (friends, families, fans, and followers). Finally, the customer buying process is becoming more social than it has been previously. Customers are paying more attention to their social circle in making decisions. They seek advice and reviews, both online and offline.

Reflection Questions

- What are the trends in your respective industry that demonstrate the shifts toward a more horizontal, inclusive, and social business landscape?

- What are your plans to embrace these shifts in the marketplace?

2 The Paradoxes of Marketing to Connected Customers

Online vs. Offline Interaction,
Informed vs. Distracted Customer, and
Negative vs. Positive Advocacy

W e have always believed that the word *marketing* should be written as *market-ing*. Writing it that way reminds us that marketing is about dealing with the ever-changing market, and that to understand cutting-edge marketing, we should understand how the market has been evolving in recent years.

The clues and trends are there for us to see. A new breed of customer, the one that will be the majority in the near future, is emerging globally—young, urban, middle-class with strong mobility and connectivity. While the mature markets are dealing with an aging population, the emerging market is enjoying the demographic dividend of a younger, more productive population. They are not only young, they are also rapidly migrating to urban areas and embracing a big-city lifestyle. The majority of them are in the middle class or above and thus have a sizable income to spend. Moving up from a lower socio-economic status, they aspire to accomplish greater goals, experience finer things, and emulate behaviors of people in higher classes. These traits make them a compelling market for marketers to pursue.

But what distinguishes this new type of customer from other markets we have seen before is their tendency to be mobile. They move around a lot, often commute, and live life at a faster pace. Everything should be instant and time-efficient. When they are interested in things they see on television, they search for them on their mobile devices. When they are deciding whether to buy something in-store, they research price and quality online. Being digital natives, they can make purchase decisions anywhere and anytime, involving a wide range of devices. Despite their internet savvy, they love to experience things physically. They value high-touch engagement when interacting with brands. They are also very social; they communicate with and trust one another. In fact, they trust their network of friends and family more than they trust corporations and brands. In short, they are highly connected.

Breaking the Myths of Connectivity

Connectivity is arguably the most important game changer in the history of marketing. Granted, it can no longer be considered a new buzzword, but it has been changing many facets of marketing and is not showing signs of slowing down.

Connectivity has made us question many mainstream theories and major assumptions that we have learned about customer, product, and brand management. Connectivity significantly reduces the costs of interaction among companies, employees, channel partners, customers, and other relevant parties. This in turn lowers the barriers to entering new markets, enables concurrent product development, and shortens the time frame for brand building.

There have been various cases of how connectivity quickly disrupted long-established industries with seemingly high entry barriers. Amazon has disrupted the brick-and-mortar bookstores and later the publishing industry. Likewise, Netflix has disturbed the brick-and-mortar video rental stores and, along with the likes of Hulu, has shaken up the satellite and cable TV services. In a similar fashion, Spotify and Apple Music have changed the way music distribution works.

Connectivity also changes the way we see the competition and customers. Today, collaboration with the competitors and co-creation with customers are central. Competition is no longer a zero-sum game. Customers are no longer the passive receivers of a company's segmentation, targeting, and positioning moves. Connectivity accelerates market dynamics to the point where it is virtually impossible for a company to stand alone and rely on internal resources to win. A company must face the reality that to win it must collaborate with external parties and even involve customer participation.

The success of Procter and Gamble's (P&G's) Connect + Develop program exemplifies this. Instead of protecting the brand equity of Febreze as its own competitive advantage, P&G licenses the trademark for new categories. Partner companies such as Kaz and Bissell launched Honeywell scented fans and odor-removing vacuum bag filters that carry the Febreze brand.

Despite the obvious influence, connectivity is often underrated as a mere application of technology that marketers need to deal with. Seeing connectivity from a technological viewpoint alone would often be misleading. In the context of strategy, many marketers view connectivity simply as an enabling platform and infrastructure that support the overall direction. A bigger-picture view of connectivity allows marketers to avoid this trap. While it is true that connectivity has been driven by technology—namely "screen technology and the internet"—its importance is far more strategic.

A survey by Google reveals that 90 percent of our interactions with media are now facilitated by screens: smartphone, tablet, laptop, and television screens. Screens are becoming so important in our lives that we spend more than four hours of our leisure time daily to use multiple screens sequentially and simultaneously. And behind these screen-based interactions, the internet has been the backbone. Global internet traffic has grown by a factor of 30 from 2000 to 2014, connecting four out of ten people in the world. According to a Cisco forecast, we will see another ten-fold jump of global internet traffic by 2019, powered by more than 11 billion connected mobile devices.

With such a massive reach, connectivity transforms the way customers behave. When shopping in-store, most customers would search for price comparison and product reviews. Google research shows that eight out of ten smartphone users in the United States do mobile research in-store. Even when watching television advertising, more than half of the TV audience in Indonesia conducts mobile search. This is a trend affecting customers globally.

Derivative products of the internet also enable transparency. Social media such as Twitter and Instagram enable customers to show and share their customer experience, which further inspires other customers from the same or a lower class to emulate and pursue a similar experience. Communal rating sites such as TripAdvisor and Yelp empower customers to make informed choices based on the wisdom of the crowd.

Thus, to fully embrace connectivity we need to view it holistically. While *mobile connectivity*—through mobile devices—is important, it is the most basic level of connectivity, in which the internet serves only as a communications infrastructure. The next level is *experiential connectivity*, in which the internet is used to deliver a superior customer experience in touchpoints between customers and brands. In this stage, we are no longer concerned only about the width but also about the depth of the connectivity. The ultimate level is *social connectivity*, which is about the strength of connection in communities of customers.

Since connectivity is closely related to the youth segment, it is also often considered relevant only for the younger generation of customers. As a result, many marketers implement "connected" marketing as a separate youth strategy without fully understanding how it fits with the overall marketing strategy. It is true that being digital natives, younger customers are the first to adopt connectivity, but they inspire their seniors to adopt connectivity as well. Moreover, as the world population ages over time, digital natives will become the majority and connectivity eventually will become the new normal.

The importance of connectivity will transcend technology and demographic segment. Connectivity changes the key foundation of marketing: the market itself.

Paradox No. 1: Online Interaction versus Offline Interaction

The impact of connectivity with regard to online and offline businesses is not clear cut. While online businesses have taken up a significant portion of the market in recent years, we do not believe that they will completely replace offline businesses. Similarly, we do not believe that the online "new wave" marketing will ultimately replace the offline "legacy" marketing. In fact, we believe that they need to coexist to deliver the best customer experience.

Here is why: in an increasingly high-tech world, high-touch interaction is becoming the new differentiation. Birchbox, an online-first beauty product retailer, opened its brick-and-mortar store to complement its existing e-commerce business. The retailer provides iPads to make personalized recommendations, mimicking its online personalization scheme. Zappos, an online shoe and clothing retailer, relies heavily on very personal call-center interactions as a winning formula. Buying shoes online can be a daunting task for many customers, but a touch of personal consultation from the call-center agents reduces the psychological barrier. Another example is Bank of America's Express Financial Centers. When making transactions on ATMs in these centers, customers can video-chat with a personal teller for assistance. The service combines ATM convenience with a personalized human touch. Even Amazon needed to create a "physical channel" with its Dash Button, which allows shoppers to automatically replenish household products such as coffee and detergent with a push of a doorbell-sized button. It is Amazon's early "internet of things" attempt to connect otherwise offline devices such as a coffee maker and a washing machine.

On the other hand, a high-tech interface can also enhance a predominantly high-touch interaction, making it more compelling. Macy's shopBeacon project is an example of this. With Apple's iBeacon transmitters installed in various locations within a Macy's store, customers will be alerted with highly targeted offerings throughout their journey in-store. When walking past a certain department, customers might be reminded of their shopping list, receive discount notifications, and get gift recommendations through an iPhone app. As transaction data accumulate over time, the offerings will become more personalized to each shopper profile. Another example is John Lewis's sofa studio, which allows customers to select a sofa model from

3-D-printed miniatures. By placing a miniature alongside a selection of fabric in front of a computer screen, customers can see what their sofa will look like on the screen. It gives a very playful customer experience when choosing sofa model and fabric.

As it turns out, the online and offline world will eventually coexist and converge. Technology touches both the online world and the off-line physical space, making it possible for the ultimate online–offline convergence. Sensor technologies, such as near field communication (NFC) and location-based iBeacon, provide a far more compelling customer experience. In the engine room, big-data analytics enables the personalization that new customers are longing for. All of these complement the traditional human interface that was the backbone of marketing before the rise of the internet.

Traditional and contemporary media for marketing communications such as television and social media will also complement each other. Many people go to Twitter for breaking news but eventually return to television and watch CNN for more credible and deeper news coverage. On the other hand, watching television is often a trigger for people to pursue online activities on their smartphones. For example, a movie showing on television might trigger an online review search. A television commercial can also be a call to action for people to buy products online.

The characters of the new customers prompt us to realize that the future of marketing will be a seamless blend of online and offline experiences across customer paths. In the beginning, brand awareness and appeal will come from a mix of analytics-powered marketing communications, past customer experiences, and recommendations from friends and family, both online and offline. Customers will then follow up through series of further research, utilizing the reviews from other customers—again online and offline. If customers decide to make a purchase, they will experience a personalized touch from both the machine and the human interface. Experienced customers will in turn become advocates for inexperienced customers. Entire experiences are recorded, which further improves the accuracy of the analytics engine.

In a highly connected world, a key challenge for brands and companies is to integrate online and offline elements into the total customer experience.

Paradox No. 2: Informed Customer versus Distracted Customer

We all think that today's customers are the most powerful. It is valid to say that most of them actively search for information on brands. They make more informed purchase decisions. But despite their higher level of curiosity and knowledge, they are not in control of what they want to buy.

In making purchase decisions, customers are essentially influenced by three factors. First, they are influenced by marketing communications in various media such as television ads, print ads, and public relations. Second, they are persuaded by the opinions of their friends and family. Third, they also have personal knowledge and an attitude about certain brands based on past experiences.

The truth is that today's customers have become highly dependent on the opinions of others. In many cases, others' words have even outweighed both personal preference and marketing communications. The reason for this is none other than the connectivity itself.

On the bright side, connectivity brings a lot of protection and confidence. In the customers' minds, their inner circle of friends and family provides protection against bad brands and companies. But connectivity, along with the presence of multiple devices and screens, also brings distractions. It hampers the customers' ability to focus and often limits their ability to decide. Thus, many customers make their decisions by following the wisdom of the crowd. This is further fueled by the low level of trust that customers put in advertising and the limited time they have to compare qualities and prices. Further, because it is very convenient to receive advice from others, the importance of word of mouth is growing in the final purchase decision.

This is the portrait of the future customers—connected yet distracted. A survey by the National Center for Biotechnological Information shows that the average human attention span has dropped from 12 seconds in 2000 to 8 seconds in 2013. This can be attributed to the massive and overwhelming volume of messages that constantly bombard our connected mobile devices and demand instant attention.

The challenge for marketers going forward is twofold. First, marketers need to win customer attention. It would be hard for a brand manager to get a customer to sit through a 30-second advertisement and for a salesperson to engage a customer using a 30-second elevator pitch. In the future, it will be more difficult to get a brand message across. Customer attention will be scarce; thus, only brands with WOW! factors will be worthwhile for them listen to and to advocate. Second, marketers need to create brand conversations in customer communities despite not having much control over the outcome. Marketers need to make sure that when customers ask others about a brand, there will be loyal advocates who sway the decision in the brand's favor.

Paradox No. 3: Negative Advocacy versus Positive Advocacy

Connectivity allows customers to express opinions that others may listen to. It changes the mindset of customers to admit that advice from strangers might be more credible than a recommendation from celebrity brand endorsers. Thus, connectivity creates a perfect environment for customer advocacy of brands.

Advocacy itself is not a new concept in marketing. Also known as "word of mouth," it has become the new definition of "loyalty" during the past decade. Customers who are considered loyal to a brand have the willingness to endorse and recommend the brand to their friends and family.

The most famous measurement of brand advocacy is arguably the Net Promoter Score designed by Frederick Reichheld. He argues that there are three broad categories of customers with regard to their attitude toward a brand: *promoters*, who recommend the brand; *passives*, who are neutral; and *detractors*, who are unlikely to recommend the brand. The Net Promoter Score is measured by the percentage of promoters subtracted from the percentage of detractors. The key argument is that the ill effect of negative word of mouth reduces the good effect of positive word of mouth.

While the concept has proven to be useful for tracking loyalty, the simple subtraction might leave behind some important insights. When a brand stays true to its DNA and consistently pursues its target segment, the brand polarizes the market. Some become lovers and others become haters of the brand. But in the context of connectivity, a negative advocacy might not necessarily be a bad thing. In reality, sometimes a brand needs negative advocacy to trigger positive advocacy from others. We argue that in many cases, without negative advocacy, positive advocacy might remain dormant.

Like brand awareness, brand advocacy can be spontaneous or it can prompted. Spontaneous brand advocacy happens when a customer, without being prompted or asked, actively recommends a particular brand. In truth, this type of advocacy is rare. One needs to be a die-hard fan to be an active advocate. Another form of advocacy is the prompted advocacy—a brand recommendation that results from a trigger by others. This type of advocacy, while very common, is dormant. When a brand has strong prompted advocacy, it needs to be activated by either customer enquiries or negative advocacy.

It is true that the balance between lovers and haters must be managed. Still, great brands do not necessarily have significantly more lovers than haters. In fact, YouGov BrandIndex reveals an interesting fact. McDonald's, for example, has 33 percent lovers and 29 percent haters, a near balanced polarization. Starbucks has a similar profile: 30

percent lovers and 23 percent haters. From the Net Promoter Score point of view, two of the biggest brands in the food and beverage industry would have very low scores because they have too many haters. But from an alternative viewpoint, the group of haters is a necessary evil that activates the group of lovers to defend McDonald's and Starbucks against criticisms. Without both positive and negative advocacy, the brand conversations would be dull and less engaging.

Any brand that has strong characters and DNA would likely be unpopular with a certain market segment. But what these brands should aim to have is the ultimate sales force: an army of lovers who are willing to guard the brand in the digital world.

Summary: Marketing amid Paradoxes

The changing landscape creates a set of paradoxes for marketers to deal with, one of which is online versus offline interaction. Both are meant to coexist and be complementary, with a common aim of delivering superior customer experience. Furthermore, there is a paradox of the informed versus the distracted customer. Even as connectivity empowers customers with abundant information, customers have also become overly dependent on others' opinions, which often outweigh personal preferences. Finally, with connectivity come enormous opportunities for brands to earn positive advocacies. Still, they are also prone to attracting negative advocacies. That may not necessarily be bad because negative advocacies often activate positive advocacies.

Reflection Questions

- What are some of the cases in your industry that capture the paradoxical nature of connected customers?
- How do you plan to embrace the paradoxes?

3 The Influential Digital Subcultures

Youth for Mind Share,
Women for Market Share, and
Netizens for Heart Share

When it comes to brand advocacy in the digital world, not all customers are created equal. Some segments rely on their own personal preferences and what they hear from advertising; thus advocacy does not matter to them. Moreover, they do not share their experience with everyone else. Other segments have a greater tendency to ask for and give recommendations on brands. They are the ones who are more likely to be loyal brand advocates.

For increased probability of getting advocacy, marketers should place their bets on youth, women, and netizens (YWN). Many topics related to these three major segments have been researched and explored separately. In terms of size, each of these is a very lucrative segment. Thus, the marketing approach has been tailored specifically to cater to them. But here is the bigger picture. There is a common thread that connects them: YWN are the most influential segments in the digital era.

It is perhaps not surprising that most subcultures—groups that have sets of norms and beliefs outside of the mainstream culture (e.g., cosplayers, homeschoolers, and hackers)—come predominantly from either youth, women, or netizens. They were, in many parts of the world, considered minorities and on the periphery of society. In the past, authority and power indeed belonged to seniors, men, and citizens. This was due to the traditionally higher level of income and purchasing power that seniors, men, and citizens have had. But over time, the importance and influence of YWN has increased significantly. In fact, the subcultures that YWN represent have begun to influence the mainstream culture. Their relatively larger networks of communities, friends, and family empower them to do this.

Youth, for example, set the trends for their seniors, especially when it comes to pop culture fields such as music, movies, sports, food, fashion, and technology. Seniors often do not have the time and agility to fully explore the fast-changing pop culture; they simply follow and rely on the recommendations of youth. Younger-generation consumers often become the first to try new products, thus often becoming the primary target market for marketers. When youth accept new products, those products usually reach the mainstream market successfully.

In many countries the women in the household act as the chief financial officer of the family. In selecting which brand to buy in many product and service categories, women's voices often trump men's. This is because most women have the patience and interest to go through a comprehensive process of researching for the best choice, something that most men consider useless or even painful. Thus, women play a significant role in becoming the gatekeeper of any products and services that marketers offer to families.

Netizens—or citizens of the internet—are also highly influential. As digital natives, they are very savvy in connecting with others online while sharing information. While not all their shared information is valuable and not all their activities are productive, they are clearly the epitome of smarter customers. Representing what they see as a true model of boundaryless democracy, they freely express their opinions and feelings about brands, often anonymously. They create ratings, post comments, and even create content that other citizens pay attention to.

Because of their characteristics, YWN are not easy to impress. But when we impress them, they will be the most loyal advocates of our brands. Brand advocacy from quality segments such as YWN is more valuable than from others. Because YWN have a strong influence on the mainstream market, brands will reap huge benefits by engaging them.

Youth: Acquiring the Mind Share

For marketers, it makes sense to target youth. According to a report by the United Nations Population Fund (UNPFA), in 2014 there were

1.8 billion young people between the ages of 10 and 24, the highest number in human history, and their number will continue to grow. Interestingly, approximately 90 percent of them are living in less-developed countries. They are facing all sorts of life challenges to realize their full potential in education and career while managing social dynamics among their peers. Marketers are identifying and solving these challenges. The goal is to be relevant to young people's lives and therefore to gain access to their growing wallets.

Even marketers whose products and services do not primarily aim at young customers pursue this lucrative market. The objective is to influence their minds early in their lives, even if it is still not profitable to do so currently. Today's young people, in the near future, will be the primary and probably the most profitable customers.

Moreover, targeting youth is the most exciting thing that marketers do. Marketing to them always involves either cool advertisements, trendy digital content, celebrity endorsements, or innovative brand activations. Unlike older segments, youth are so dynamic that it is rarely unproductive to engage them. And since the demographic size is huge, companies are often willing to spend heavily on this interesting marketing segment.

The role of youth in influencing the rest of the market is immense. First, they are *early adopters.* Youth are often accused of being rebellious and anti-establishment—that is, they love what adults hate. Although some youth are behaving as accused, most of them are not. The truth is that youth are just not afraid of experimentation. They try new products and experience new services that older segments deem too risky.

Marketers with newly developed and launched products need them. A youth-first strategy often has the highest likelihood of success. When the iPod was first introduced in 2001, the youth-oriented tonality of its advertising helped create rapid early adoption and eventually mainstream market success. Similarly, when Netflix offered its streaming-only service in 2010, its early adopters were tech-savvy youth.

Secondly, youth are *trendsetters*. Youth are the Now Generation customers who demand instant everything. When it comes to trends, they are very agile. They follow trends so fast that marketers often fail to keep up. But the upside is that this allows marketers to quickly pinpoint trends that will influence the market in the near future.

Their tribal nature means that youth are also very fragmented. Thus, trends that youth follow are equally fragmented. Certain sports, music, and fashion trends might have cult following among some youth tribes but might not be relevant for others. Perhaps the only trend that most youth follow is the movement toward a digital lifestyle.

While many youth-endorsed trends turn out to be short-lived fads due to this fragmentation, some evolving trends do manage to hit the mainstream. The rise of Justin Bieber, who initially gained fame as a trending YouTube artist followed by millions of youth, is an example. The entire universe of social media, such as Facebook and Twitter, also started out as a trend among youth. Similarly, music-streaming services such as Spotify, Apple Music, and Joox were brought to the mainstream market by young customers.

Finally, youth are *game changers*. They are often associated with irresponsible and selfish behaviors. But recent trends show that they are maturing much earlier. This is because young people respond more quickly to changes happening in the world, such as globalization and technological advances. Now, they are concerned about what is happening around them. In fact, they are one of the primary drivers of change in the world.

We can see this from the growing youth empowerment movements. RockCorps, for instance, is a platform that allows youth to volunteer for four hours to transform communities and earn one ticket to an exclusive concert. Another example is WE.org, which invites young people to participate in world-changing events such as a series of inspiring "WE Day" live concerts, as well as to purchase "ME to WE" products that have social impact. Indonesia Mengajar offers a similar empowerment platform through education. It rigorously selects the country's top graduates, asking them to forgo potentially high-paying jobs in favor of teaching in remote village schools for one year. These movements make volunteering look cool. More importantly, this program raises the awareness of older generations about the importance of activism and social impact.

These roles—early adopters, trend setters, and game changers—all lead to the conclusion that youth are the key to *mind-share.* If brands want to influence the minds of mainstream customers, convincing youth is the important first step.

Women: Growing the Market Share

The female market is also a logical one for marketers to pursue. Not only is its size enormous, the segment profile is also distinctive. Highlighting the psychological differences, John Gray metaphorically argues that "men are from Mars, women are from Venus."

The inherent differences between men and women have been a subject for both psychology and marketing. Many experts have put forth their views about marketing to women. Many products, services, and marketing campaigns have been developed specifically for women.

The influence that women have on others is defined by what they do. Rena Bartos, in her book *Marketing to Women Around the World,* describes the segmentation of the female market: stay-at-home housewife, plan-to-work housewife, working woman with a job, or career woman. To put it simply, the world of women revolves around family and work. The dilemma they often face is either to choose one alternative or to balance between family and career. But being more suited to multitasking, women are inherently better managers when it comes to complex, multifaceted assignments, at home, at work, or both.

In general, there are three roles that women play. First of all, women are *information collectors.* According to Martha Barletta, a woman's decision-making process differs from a man's. Whereas a man's path-to-purchase is short and straightforward, a woman's resembles a spiral, often going back to previous steps to collect new information and to reassess whether moving to the next step is the right choice. Women typically spend hours in stores reviewing quality and comparing prices as well as hours researching online, while men typically limit their search and go after what they want as quickly as possible.

Not only do women research more, they also converse more about brands. They seek out the opinions of their friends and family, and they are open to receiving assistance from others. While men just want to get things done, women want to find the perfect product, the perfect service, or the perfect solution.

For marketers, the information-collecting nature of women has its benefits. It means that all marketing communications and customer education efforts are not a waste. Women actually pay attention to all the information, and they will eventually summarize it for others.

In relation to that, women are *holistic shoppers.* The fact that they experience more touchpoints in their spiral path-to-purchase means that they are exposed to more factors for consideration. They are more likely to consider everything—functional benefits, emotional benefits, prices, and the like—before determining the true value of products and services. For certain household categories, women consider products' value not only to themselves but to the entire family.

Women also consider and browse for more brands, including less popular brands that they believe might have more value. Because of this, women are more confident about their choice when they finally buy. Thus, they are more loyal and more inclined to recommend their choice to their community.

Because of these aforementioned qualities, women are de facto *household managers.* They deserve the titles of chief financial officer, purchasing manager, and asset manager of the family. Not only are they the gatekeepers for most household products, including big-ticket items, women are also the influencers for other products such as investment and financial services.

A Pew Research Center report in 2008 revealed that in 41 percent of U.S. households, women were the ones calling the shots whereas in only 26 percent of the households, men were more dominant (in the remainder of the households, they equally split decision making). In Indonesia, the picture is even more striking. Based on a survey by MarkPlus Insight in 2015, about 74 percent of Indonesian women managed all the family finances—controlling even the income of their spouses—although only 51 percent of them were working.

It turns out that the role that women play at home is spreading to the workplace. In 2013, the U.S. Bureau of Labor Statistics reported that women account for 41 percent of the employees who have the authority to make purchasing decisions for their employers in the United States.

The influence of women at home and at work is growing. As information collectors, holistic shoppers, and household managers, women are the key to win *market share* in the digital economy. To access even bigger markets, brands will need to get past women's comprehensive decision-making process.

Netizens: Expanding the Heart Share

Michael Hauben, who coined the word in the early 1990s, defines *netizens* as the people across geographical boundaries who care about and actively work toward developing the internet for the benefit of the larger world.

Netizens are considered to be the true citizens of democracy because they want to be involved in the development of the internet. They see the world horizontally, not vertically. The content on the internet is created and shared by the people and for the people. But they believe in total democracy and not so much in governance. They embrace openness and sharing with others with no geographical boundaries.

There are 3.4 billion internet users—45 percent of the world's population, according to United Nations estimates. Not all of them can be considered netizens or citizens of the Internet. Forrester's Social Technographics segmentation can help explain why not all internet users deserve to be called netizens. According to the segmentation, there is a hierarchy of internet users, including inactives, spectators (people who watch and read online content), joiners (people who join and visit social media), collectors (people who add tags to webpages and use RSS feeds), critics (people who post ratings and comments online), and creators (people who create and publish online content). The collectors, critics, and creators best characterize the netizens— people who actively contribute to the internet and do not just consume on the internet.

Their role in influencing others is related to their desire to always be connected and to contribute. Netizens are *social connectors*. We know that netizens love to connect. They talk to one another, and information flows as they converse. Under anonymity, they have fewer risks and therefore are more confident when interacting with others and participating in online conversations. On the internet, their user-names and avatars are their identities.

There are many ways to socially connect on the internet. The most popular are social networking services and instant messaging apps such as Facebook, WhatsApp, QQ, Tumblr, Instagram, and LinkedIn. A relationship on those platforms usually starts as a one-to-one connection between two individuals who know and trust each other. This initial connection will lead to a link between the two individuals' separate networks, creating a many-to-many connection. From the outside, online communities look like webs of strangers, but on the inside, they are webs of trusting friends. Since it is a many-to-many network built on one-to-one relationships, an internet community usually grows exponentially and becomes one of the strongest forms of community.

Netizens are also *expressive evangelists.* Not revealing their true identities, internet users can be very aggressive in expressing their opinions. The negative side of this is the emergence of cyberbullies, trolls, and haters on the internet. The positive side, however, is the emergence of brand evangelists. Netizens, unlike internet users in general, are more likely to be brand evangelists.

In the internet world, we know the f-factors: followers, fans, and friends. When they are passionate about and emotionally committed to a brand, netizens become the f-factors. They become evangelists or lovers, as opposed to haters, of the brand. Sometimes dormant, they often become active when they need to safeguard their favorite brand against cyberbullies, trolls, and haters.

Further, evangelists are also storytellers of the brand who spread the news about brands to their networks. They tell authentic stories from a customer's point of view—a role that advertising can never replace. As netizens who are more high-profile than other internet users, they yield a huge influence, often having a large number of their own followers, fans, and friends.

Netizens are also *content contributors.* They are called the internet citizens for a reason. Like good citizens contributing to their country, they contribute to the development of the internet. The work of netizens makes life easier for other internet users. With the use of tags, information on the internet is better organized and quality content becomes easier for others to search. By "voting" for websites, netizens recommend quality websites to others. With product ratings and reviews on the internet, other users can easily discover the best available choice.

The most important contribution, however, is to create new content, which can be in multiple formats: articles, whitepapers, e-books, infographics, graphic arts, games, videos, and even movies. Independent authors write Web pages, blogs, and e-books. Independent musicians and moviemakers create commercial hits by becoming YouTubers and creating content on the video-sharing platform.

With new content being created every second, the internet is becoming richer and more useful, which will benefit users and draw non-users to start using the internet. All these grow the netizen population as well as the value of the internet.

Growing exponentially on the basis of emotional and mutually beneficial connections, communities of netizens are the key to expand a brand's heart share. When it comes to communal word of mouth, netizens are the best amplifiers. A brand message will flow along social connections if it receives the netizens' seal of approval.

Summary: Youth, Women, and Netizens

Youth, women, and netizens have long been researched thoroughly by businesses but typically as separate customer segments. Their collective strength, especially as the most influential segments in the digital era, has not quite been explored. Youth are early adopters of new products and technologies. They are also trend setters, yet are fragmented as to the trends they follow. Ultimately they are game changers. As information collectors and holistic shoppers, women are de facto household managers, the chief financial officer, purchase manager, and asset manager all rolled into one. Finally, netizens are social connectors, as they overwhelmingly connect, converse, and communicate with their peers. They are also expressive evangelists as well as content contributors in the online world. Together, youth, women, and netizens hold the key to marketing in the digital economy.

Reflection Questions

- How can your business acquire greater mind share by leveraging youth's roles of early adopters and trendsetters?

- How can your business grow market share by leveraging the household influence of women?

- How can your business identify and utilize netizens to win greater heart share?

4 Marketing 4.0 in the Digital Economy

When Online Meets Offline,
Style Meets Substance, and
Machine-to-Machine Meets Human-to-Human

According to the Organization for Economic Cooperation and Development (OECD), digital innovations can bring countries closer to sustainable prosperity. McKinsey lists top innovations that have had the most significant economic impact, including mobile internet, automation of knowledge work, the internet of things, cloud technology, advanced robotics, and 3-D printing, among others. These digital technologies have been around for some years but their impact reached the highest point only recently, fueled by the convergence of multiple technologies.

These technologies help develop multiple sectors in the economy such as retail (e-commerce), transportation (automated vehicles), education (massive open online courses), health (electronic record and personalized medicine), as well as social interactions (social networks). However, many of the same technologies that drive the digital economy are also disrupting key industries and upsetting major incumbents. Large retailers such as Borders and Blockbuster, for instance, experienced the disruptions caused by digitally empowered entrants in their respective industries. These digitally empowered entrants—Amazon and Netflix—are now the new major incumbents in their industries. Interestingly, even the past disrupters may experience the same fate. Apple's iTunes, which once successfully disrupted the brick-and-mortar music retailers with its online music retailing, has been disrupted by Spotify and its music-streaming business model. Apple's revenue from music sales has been in decline since its peak in the early 2000s. Apple launched its own music-streaming service, Apple Music, in mid-2015 to rival Spotify.

Adapting to the emerging disruptive technologies, most customers are excited and anxious at the same time. Automation of knowledge work, for example, has not only bumped up productivity but has also brought fears of losing jobs. 3-D printing has opened a world of possibilities in terms of rapid innovation. But on the negative side, 3-D printing can also be misused for producing guns, for example.

The most significant dilemma is perhaps caused by the mobile internet. It has brought peer-to-peer connectivity and empowered customers to be much smarter and better informed than in the past. But a study by Przybylski and Weinstein of the University of Essex proved that mobile phones may also hurt relationships. The research revealed that mobile phones divert people's attention away from their current environments. It also discovered that the feeling of being able to connect to a wider network often inhibits people's abilities to be empathetic to others nearby. Therefore, as the drive toward digital economy intensifies, customers are longing for the perfect application of technologies that allows them to self-actualize while becoming empathetic at the same time.

In this transition and adaptation period to the digital economy, a new marketing approach is required to guide marketers in anticipating and leveraging the disruptive technologies. For the past six years, marketers have been asking for a sequel to *Marketing 3.0: From Products to Customers to the Human Spirit* (Wiley, 2010). Our book was so universally accepted that it was translated into 24 non-English languages. In the book, we talked about the major shift from product-driven marketing (1.0) to customer-centric marketing (2.0) to ultimately human-centric marketing (3.0).

We now want to introduce Marketing 4.0. Marketing 4.0 is a marketing approach that combines online and offline interaction between companies and customers. In the digital economy, digital interaction alone is not sufficient. In fact, in an increasingly online world, offline touch represents a strong differentiation. Marketing 4.0 also blends style with substance. While it is imperative for brands to be more flexible and adaptive due to rapid technological trends, their authentic characters are more important than ever. In an increasingly transparent world, authenticity is the most valuable asset. Finally,

Marketing 4.0 leverages machine-to-machine connectivity and artificial intelligence to improve marketing productivity while leveraging human-to-human connectivity to strengthen customer engagement.

Moving from Traditional to Digital Marketing

From Segmentation and Targeting to Customer Community Confirmation

Traditionally, marketing always starts with segmentation—a practice of dividing the market into homogenous groups based on their geographic, demographic, psychographic, and behavioral profiles. Segmentation is typically followed by targeting—a practice of selecting one or more segments that a brand is committed to pursue based on their attractiveness and fit with the brand. Segmentation and targeting are both fundamental aspects of a brand's strategy. They allow for efficient resource allocation and sharper positioning. They also help marketers to serve multiple segments, each with differentiated offerings.

However, segmentation and targeting also exemplify the vertical relationship between a brand and its customers, analogous to hunter and prey. Segmentation and targeting are unilateral decisions made by marketers without the consent of their customers. Marketers determine the variables that define the segments. The involvement of customers is limited to their inputs in market research, which usually precede segmentation and targeting exercises. Being "targets," customers often feel intruded upon and annoyed by irrelevant messages aimed toward them. Many consider one-way messages from brands to be spam.

In the digital economy, customers are socially connected with one another in horizontal webs of communities. Today, *communities* are the new *segments*. Unlike segments, communities are naturally formed by customers within the boundaries that they themselves define. Customer communities are immune to spamming and irrelevant advertising. In fact, they will reject a company's attempt to force its way into these webs of relationship.

To effectively engage with a community of customers, brands must ask for permission. Permission marketing, introduced by Seth Godin, revolves around this idea of asking for customers' consent prior to delivering marketing messages. However, when asking for permission, brands must act as friends with sincere desires to help, not hunters with bait. Similar to the mechanism on Facebook, customers will have the decision to either "confirm" or "ignore" the friend requests. This demonstrates the horizontal relationship between brands and customers. However, companies may continue to use segmentation, targeting, and positioning as long as it is made transparent to customers.

From Brand Positioning and Differentiation to Brand Clarification of Characters and Codes

In a traditional sense, a brand is a set of images—most often a name, a logo, and a tagline—that distinguishes a company's product or service offering from its competitors'. It also serves as a reservoir that stores all the value generated by the company's brand campaigns. In recent years, a brand has also become the representation of the overall customer experience that a company delivers to its customers. Therefore, a brand may serve as a platform for a company's strategy since any activities that the company engages in will be associated with the brand.

The concept of *brand* is closely linked with *brand positioning*. Since the 1980s, brand positioning has been recognized as the battle for the customer's mind. To establish strong equity, a brand must have a clear and consistent positioning as well as an authentic set of differentiation to support the positioning. Brand positioning is essentially a compelling promise that marketers convey to win the customers' minds and hearts. To exhibit true brand integrity and win customers' trust, marketers must fulfill this promise with a solid and concrete differentiation through its marketing mix.

In the digital economy, customers are now facilitated and empowered to evaluate and even scrutinize any company's brand-positioning promise. With this transparency (due to the rise of social media) brands can no longer make false, unverifiable promises. Companies can position themselves as anything, but unless there is essentially a community-driven consensus the positioning amounts to nothing more than corporate posturing.

Today, consistently communicating brand identity and positioning in a repetitive manner—a key success factor in traditional marketing—may no longer be enough. With disruptive technologies, shorter product life cycles, and rapidly changing trends, a brand must be dynamic enough to behave in certain ways in certain situations. What should remain consistent, however, are the brand characters and codes. The character is the brand's raison d'être, its authentic reason for being. When the core of the brand remains true to its roots, the outer imagery can be flexible. Think of it this way: by having countless logo adaptations—Google calls them doodles—MTV and Google remain solid yet flexible as brands.

From Selling the Four P's to Commercializing the Four C's

The marketing mix is a classic tool to help plan *what to offer* and *how to offer* to the customers. Essentially, there are four P's: product, price, place, and promotion. Product is often developed based on customers' needs and wants, captured through market research. Companies control the majority of product decisions from conception to production. To establish a selling price for the product, companies use a combination of cost-based, competition-based, and customer value–

based pricing methods. Customers' willingness to pay, estimated in consumer value–based pricing, is the most important input that customers have in connection with pricing.

Once companies decide *what to offer* (product and price), they need to decide *how to offer* (place and promotion). Companies need to determine where to distribute the product with the objective of making it conveniently available and accessible to customers. Companies also need to communicate the information about the product to the target audience through various methods such as advertising, public relations, and sales promotions. When the four P's of the marketing mix are optimally designed and aligned, selling becomes less challenging as customers are attracted to the value propositions.

In a connected world, the concept of marketing mix has evolved to accommodate more customer participation. Marketing mix (the four P's) should be redefined as the four C's (co-creation, currency, communal activation, and conversation).

In the digital economy, co-creation is the new product development strategy. Through co-creation and involving customers early in the ideation stage, companies can improve the success rate of new product development. Co-creation also allows customers to customize and personalize products and services, thereby creating superior value propositions.

The concept of pricing is also evolving in the digital era from standardized to dynamic pricing. Dynamic pricing—setting flexible prices based on market demand and capacity utilization—is not new in some industries such as hospitality and airlines. But advancement in technology has brought the practice to other industries. Online retailers, for instance, collect a massive amount of data, which allows them to perform big-data analytics and in turn to offer a unique pricing for each customer. With dynamic pricing, companies can optimize profitability by charging different customers differently based on historical purchase patterns, proximity to store locations, and other customer-profile aspects. In the digital economy, price is similar to currency, which fluctuates depending on market demand.

The concept of channel is also changing. In the sharing economy, the most potent distribution concept is peer-to-peer distribution. Players such as Airbnb, Uber, Zipcar, and Lending Club are disrupting the hotel, taxi, auto rental, and banking industries, respectively. They provide customers easy access to the products and services not owned by them but by other customers. The rise of 3-D printing will spur this peer-to-peer distribution even more in the near future. Imagine customers wanting a product and in a matter of minutes receiving the product printed in front of them. In a connected world, customers demand access to products and services almost instantly, which can only be served with their peers in close proximity. This is the essence of communal activation.

The concept of promotion has also evolved in recent years. Traditionally, promotion has always been a one-sided affair, with companies sending messages to customers as audiences. Today, the proliferation of social media enables customers to respond to those messages. It also allows customers to converse about the messages with other customers. The rise of customer-rating systems such as TripAdvisor and Yelp provide a platform for customers to have conversations about and offer evaluations of brands they have interacted with.

With a connected marketing mix (the four C's) companies have a high likelihood of surviving in the digital economy. However, the paradigm of selling needs to change as well. Traditionally, customers are passive objects of selling techniques. In a connected world, the idea is to have both sides actively obtain commercial value. With increased customer participation, companies are engaging customers in transparent commercialization.

From Customer Service Processes to Collaborative Customer Care

Prior to purchase, customers are treated as targets. Once they decide to buy, they are considered kings in a traditional customer-service perspective. Shifting to the customer-care approach, companies view customers as equals. Instead of serving customers, a company demonstrates its genuine concern for the customer by listening, responding, and consistently following through on terms dictated by both the company and the customer.

In traditional customer-service, personnel are responsible for performing specific roles and processes according to strict guidelines and standard operating procedures. This situation often puts service personnel in a dilemma over conflicting objectives. In a connected world, collaboration is the key to customer-care success. Collaboration happens when companies invite customers to participate in the process by using self-service facilities.

Integrating Traditional and Digital Marketing

Digital marketing is not meant to replace traditional marketing. Instead, the two should coexist with interchanging roles across the customer path (details about customer path are provided in Chapter 5). In the early stage of interaction between companies and customers,

Figure 4.1 The Interchanging Roles of Traditional and Digital Marketing

traditional marketing plays a major role in building awareness and interest. As the interaction progresses and customers demand closer relationships with companies, digital marketing rises in importance. The most important role of digital marketing is to drive action and advocacy. Since digital marketing is more accountable than traditional marketing, its focus is to drive results whereas traditional marketing's focus is on initiating customer interaction. (See Figure 4.1.)

The essence of Marketing 4.0 is to recognize the shifting roles of traditional and digital marketing in building customer engagement and advocacy.

Summary: Redefining Marketing in the Digital Economy

Marketing 4.0 is a marketing approach that combines online and offline interaction between companies and customers, blends style with substance in building brands, and ultimately complements machine-to-machine connectivity with human-to-human touch to strengthen customer engagement. It helps marketers to transition into the digital economy, which has redefined the key concepts of marketing. Digital marketing and traditional marketing are meant to coexist in Marketing 4.0 with the ultimate goal of winning customer advocacy.

Reflection Questions

- How can your brand develop a powerful differentiation based on human-to-human touch in the digital world?

- How can your business transition from the traditional four P's to the digital four C's by adopting co-creation, taking advantage of currency-like pricing, engaging in communal activation, and driving conversation?

- What are the fundamental changes required in your customer-service strategy to embrace collaborative customer care?

Part II
New Frameworks for Marketing in the Digital Economy

5 The New Customer Path

Aware, Appeal, Ask, Act, and Advocate

With increased mobility and connectivity, customers already have limited time to consider and evaluate brands. As the pace of life accelerates and their attention span drops, customers experience difficulty in focusing. But across multiple channels—online and offline—customers continue to be exposed to too much of everything: product features, brand promises, and sales talk. Confused by too-good-to-be-true advertising messages, customers often ignore them and instead turn to trustworthy sources of advice: their social circle of friends and family.

Companies need to realize that more touchpoints and higher volume in messages do not necessarily translate into increased influence. Companies need to stand out from the crowd and meaningfully connect with customers in just a few critical touchpoints. In fact, just one moment of unexpected delight from a brand is all it takes to transform a customer into the brand's loyal advocate. To be able to do so, companies should map the customer path to purchase, understand customer touchpoints across the path, and intervene in select touchpoints that matter. They should focus their efforts—intensifying communications, strengthening channel presence, and improving customer interface—to improve those critical touchpoints as well as to introduce strong differentiation.

Moreover, companies need to leverage the power of customer connectivity and advocacy. Nowadays, peer-to-peer conversation among customers is the most effective form of media. Given this lack of trust, companies might no longer have direct access to target customers. As customers trust their peers more than ever, the best source of influence is the army of customers turned advocates. Thus, the ultimate goal is to delight customers and convert them into loyal advocates.

Understanding How People Buy: From Four A's to Five A's

One of the earliest and widely used frameworks to describe the customer path is AIDA: *attention, interest, desire*, and *action.*
Unsurprisingly, AIDA was coined by an advertising and sales pioneer, E. St. Elmo Lewis, and was first adopted in the fields of advertising and sales. It serves as a simple checklist or a reminder for advertising executives when they design advertisements and for sales executives when they approach prospects. The advertising copy and sales pitch should grab attention, initiate interest, strengthen desire, and ultimately drive action. Similar to the four P's of marketing (product, price, place, and promotion), AIDA has undergone several expansions and modifications.

Derek Rucker of the Kellogg School of Management offers a modification of AIDA that he calls the four A's: *aware, attitude, act*, and *act again.* In this more recent framework, the *interest* and *desire* stages are simplified into *attitude* and a new stage, *act again*, is added. The modified framework aims to track post-purchase customer behavior and measure customer retention. It considers an action of repurchase as a strong proxy for customer loyalty.

The four A's framework is a simple model to describe the straightforward funnel-like process that customers go through when evaluating brands in their consideration sets. Customers learn about a brand (*aware*), like or dislike the brand (*attitude*), decide whether to purchase it (*act*), and decide whether the brand is worth a repeat purchase (*act again*). When it is treated as a customer funnel, the number of customers going through the process continues to decline as they move into the next stage. People who like the brand must have known the brand before. People who purchase the brand must have liked the brand before. And so on. Similarly, when treated as a brand funnel, the number of brands that are being considered along the path continues to decline. For example, the number of brands people recommend is less than the number of brands people buy, which in turn is less than the number of brands people know.

The four A's also reflects a primarily personal path. The major influence on customers' decision making as they move across the path comes from companies' touchpoints (e.g., TV advertising at the *aware* phase, salesperson at the *act* phase, service center at the *act again* phase). This is within a company's control.

Today, in the era of connectivity, the straightforward and personal funnel-like process of the four A's needs an update. A new customer path must be defined to accommodate changes shaped by connectivity.

- In the pre-connectivity era, an individual customer determined his or her own *attitude* toward a brand. In the connectivity era, the initial *appeal* of a brand is influenced by the community surrounding the customer to determine the final attitude. Many seemingly personal decisions are essentially social decisions. The new customer path should reflect the rise of such social influence.

- In the pre-connectivity era, loyalty was often defined as retention and repurchase. In the connectivity era, loyalty is ultimately defined as the willingness to advocate a brand. A customer might not need to continuously repurchase a particular brand (e.g., due to a longer purchase cycle) or might not be able to (e.g., due to unavailability in certain locations). But if the customer is happy with the brand, he or she will be willing to recommend it even when currently not using it. The new customer path should be aligned to this new definition of loyalty.

- When it comes to understanding brands, customers now actively connect with one another, building ask-and-advocate relationships. Netizens, in particular, have very active connections in customer forums. Customers who need more information will search for it and connect with other customers with better knowledge and more experience. Depending on the bias shown during the conversation, the connection either strengthens or weakens the brand's initial appeal. The new customer path should also recognize this connectivity among customers.

Based on these requirements, the customer path should be rewritten as the five A's: *aware, appeal, ask, act,* and *advocate.* (See Figure 5.1.)

In the *aware* phase, customers are passively exposed to a long list of brands from past experience, marketing communications, and/or the advocacy of others. This is the gateway to the entire customer path. A customer who has previous experience with a brand will likely be able to recall and recognize the brand. Advertising driven by companies and word of mouth by other customers is also a major source of brand awareness.

Aware of several brands, customers then process all the messages they are exposed to—creating short-term memory or amplifying long-term memory—and become attracted only to a short list of brands. This is the *appeal* phase. Memorable brands—with wow factors—are more likely to enter and even go higher on the short list. In highly competitive

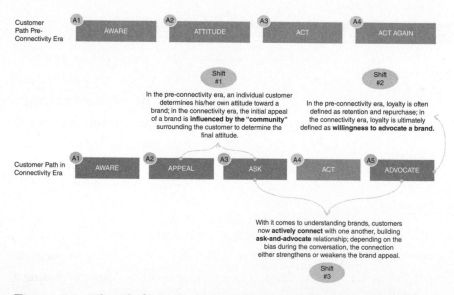

Figure 5.1 The Shifting Customer Path in a Connected World

industries where brands are abundant and products are commoditized (e.g., the consumer packaged goods categories), brand appeal must be stronger. Some customers respond to brand appeal more than others. Youth, for example, are usually among the first to respond. That is why they are more likely to be early adopters of new products.

Prompted by their curiosity, customers usually follow up by actively researching the brands they are attracted to for more information from friends and family, from the media, and/or directly from the brands. This is the *ask* stage. Customers can either call friends for advice or evaluate the short list themselves. When they decide to research some brands further, they might search online product reviews. They might also contact call centers and talk to sales agents for more information. They might also compare prices and even try out products at stores. Today, the *ask* is further complicated by the integration of the digital (online) and physical (offline) worlds. As customers browse through products in-store, they might also search for information on their mobiles. Since customers may go to multiple channels for more information, companies need to have a presence at least in the most popular channels.

At the *ask* stage, the customer path changes from individual to social. Decisions will be made based on what customers take away from the conversation with others. The brand appeal needs confirmation from others to allow the path to continue. Brands need to trigger the right amount of customer curiosity. When the curiosity level is too low, it means that the brand appeal, although existent, is rather low. But when the curiosity level is too high and customers are "forced" to ask too many questions, customers are confused about the initial message they encounter.

If they are convinced by further information in the *ask* stage, customers will decide to *act*. It is important to remember that the desired customer actions are not limited to purchase actions. After purchasing a particular brand, customers interact more deeply through consumption and usage as well as post-purchase services. Brands need to engage customers and make sure that their total ownership and usage experience is positive and memorable. When customers have problems and complaints, brands need to pay attention and make sure the customers receive solutions.

Over time, customers may develop a sense of strong loyalty to the brand, as reflected in retention, repurchase, and ultimately advocacy to others. This is the *advocate* stage. Active advocates spontaneously recommend brands they love without being asked. They tell positive stories to others and become evangelists. But most loyal advocates are passive and dormant. They need to be prompted by either a query or a negative advocacy. When they do encounter such a prompt, they feel obliged to recommend and defend the brands they love. Since loyal advocates take risks to recommend certain brands, they are also more likely to buy more of those brands in the future. (See Figure 5.2.)

The stages in the five A's are not always straightforward and are sometimes even spiral, similar to the way women buy. With attention

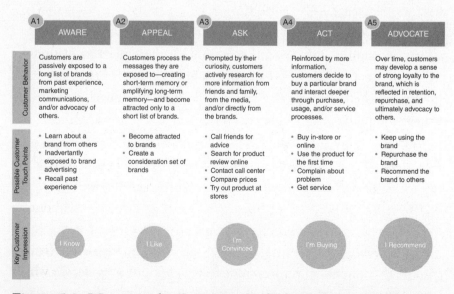

Figure 5.2 Mapping the Customer Path throughout the Five A's

deficit, customers might skip a certain phase along the customer path. For instance, a customer might not be attracted to a brand at first, but a recommendation from a friend drives the customer to eventually purchase the brand. It means that the customer skips *appeal* and goes directly from *aware* to *ask*. On the other hand, it is also possible that some customers skip *ask* and impulsively *act* solely based on the initial awareness and appeal.

In other cases (e.g., in scarce and highly popular categories), loyal advocates might not necessarily be actual buyers. Tesla products, for example, are well advocated by non-buyers. This means that customers skip *act* and go directly to *advocate*. The new customer path is not necessarily a fixed customer funnel, and customers do not necessarily go through all the five A's. Thus, from *aware* to *advocate*, the path might expand or narrow in terms of the number of customers going through each stage.

The new customer path might also be a spiral, in which customers return to previous stages, creating a feedback loop. A customer who asks questions might add new brands to the "awareness list" or find a particular brand much more appealing. A customer who encounters product issues during usage might research more about the product before deciding whether to keep using it or to switch to another. Since the path might be a spiral, the number of brands considered throughout the customer path might also fluctuate across the five A's.

The time customers spend on their path to purchase also varies across industry categories depending on the perceived importance of the categories. In consumer goods categories, for example, *aware* and *appeal* occur almost simultaneously. Thus, strong brand awareness without equally strong brand appeal in those categories usually leads to nothing. The time spent on *ask* is also typically very short. Spontaneous discovery is very common. Customers instantly and impulsively decide which brands to choose as they stroll down the grocery aisles. Most customers catch only a glimpse of each considered brand in-store and typically do not research further. For big-ticket items such as real estate and cars, on the other hand, customers are willing to spend more time asking questions and doing extensive research before purchasing the items.

The five A's framework is a flexible tool that is applicable to all industries. When used to describe customer behavior, it draws a picture that is closer to the actual customer path. It allows for cross-industry comparisons, which reveal insights into industry characteristics. It also provides insights into a company's relationship with customers in comparison with its competitors. When a company, for example, finds that the most common path its customers often take is very different from the typical customer path in its industry, the company might discover either an authentic differentiation or a hidden customer experience problem.

Driving from Awareness to Advocacy: The O Zone (O$_3$)

The ultimate goal of Marketing 4.0 is to drive customers from *awareness* to *advocacy*. In general, there are three main sources of influence marketers can use to do so. A customer's decisions across the five A's are usually influenced by a combination of their *own* influence, *others'* influence, and *outer* influence. Let us call them the O Zone (O$_3$). (See Figure 5.3.)

The *outer* influence comes from external sources. It is purposely initiated by brands through advertising and other marketing

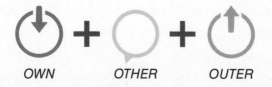

OWN   OTHER   OUTER

Figure 5.3 The O Zone of Driving Customers from Awareness to Advocacy

communications. It may also come from other customer interfaces such as sales force and customer service staff. From a brand's standpoint, *outer* influence is still manageable and controllable. The message, the media, and the frequency can be planned. The overall customer touchpoints can be designed, although the resulting customer perceptions may still vary depending on how satisfactory the experience is.

Similarly, *others'* influence also comes from the external environment. Typically, it comes from a close circle of friends and family as word of mouth. *Others'* influence can also come from a broader but independent community to which customers belong. For example, customers may be influenced by conversations they heard on social networking platforms. Customers may also be influenced by communal rating systems such as TripAdvisor and Yelp. Not all sources of *others'* influence are equal. Among many segments, the youth, women, and netizens (YWN) are the most influential. *Others'* influence coming from them is often the major driver of purchase.

Despite a brand's effort, it is essentially difficult to manage and control the outcome of *others'* influence. The only way for a brand to do so is through community marketing. Companies cannot directly control the conversation within the community, but they may facilitate discussion with the help of loyal customers.

On the other hand, *own* influence comes from within oneself. It is a result of past experience and interaction with several brands, personal judgment and evaluation of the brands, and ultimately individual preference toward the chosen brand(s). Often, personal preference (*own*) is swayed toward certain brands by word of mouth (*others'*) and advertising (*outer*). Indeed, the three major sources of influence are always intertwined.

Outer influence often reaches customers first. If a brand successfully triggers conversation with *Outer* influence, it is usually followed by *others'* influence. Ultimately, the way these two sources of influence interact will shape customers' *own* influence.

Any particular customer is usually influenced by all three types, albeit with different proportions. Some customers have stronger personal preferences and are not influenced too much by an advertisement or a friend's recommendation. Some rely heavily on the recommendation of others, and some believe in the advertisers. Despite individual variations, today's customers rely more on *others'* influence than their *own* and *outer* influence for reasons we have already discussed. Research by Nielsen in 2015 reveals that 83 percent of respondents in 60 countries rely on friends and family as the most trusted source of "advertising," and 66 percent pay attention to the opinions of others posted online.

Across the five A's, customers are most open to influence during the *ask* and *act* stages. In *ask*, customers seek advice and absorb as much information as possible from *others'* and *outer* influence with regard to a short list of brands. The *ask* stage serves as a window of opportunity for marketers to increase brand favorability. In *act*, customers shape their *own* perception of brands over time. Since they are no longer wary of *outer* pressure to buy at this stage, they have an open mindset. Brands that offer stronger customer experience during consumption and usage will be the preferred brands. (See Figure 5.4.)

The level of experience that customers have also determines their customer path. First-time buyers of a product category typically go through the entire five A's and rely a lot on *outer* influence. Thus, many first-time buyers end up buying brands with the highest share of voice.

As they become more experienced after a few rounds of purchase, they rely more on *others'*, sometimes skip the *appeal* stage, and perhaps switch brands. The most experienced customers usually have stronger *own* influence. When they have finally found their favorite brands, they will skip most stages in the five A's and continue to use the brands perpetually until the brands disappoint them.

The O_3 is another tool that helps marketers to optimize their marketing efforts. When marketers manage to identify the importance

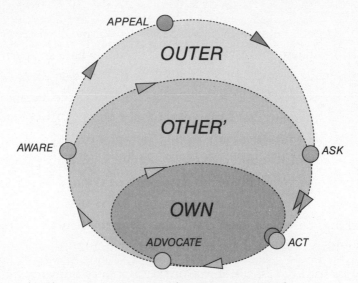

Figure 5.4 The O Zone across the Customer Path

of *outer*, *others'*, and *own* influence, they will be able to decide which activities to focus on. When *outer* influence is more important than the rest, marketers can focus more on marketing communications activities. On the other hand, when *others'* influence is the most important, marketers should rely on community marketing activities. But when *own* influence is the most important, marketers should put more emphasis on building the post-purchase customer experience.

Summary: Aware, Appeal, Ask, Act, and Advocate

In the digital economy, customer path should be redefined as the five A's—*aware*, *appeal*, *ask*, *act*, and *advocate*—which reflect the connectivity among customers. The concept of Marketing 4.0 ultimately aims to drive customers from awareness to advocacy. In doing so, marketers should leverage three main sources of influence—*own*, *others'*, and *outer* influence. This is what we call the O Zone (O_3), a useful tool that can help marketers optimize their marketing efforts.

Reflection Questions

- How can your brand identify and leverage the most critical touchpoints in the customer path?

- How can your business improve brand favorability and optimize marketing efforts by evaluating the three main sources of influence across the customer path?

6 Marketing Productivity Metrics

Purchase Action Ratio (PAR) and Brand Advocacy Ratio (BAR)

We all acknowledge the importance of brand awareness as the gate to the customer path. But too often we see marketers in various industries battling it out to achieve top-of-mind brand awareness, only to falter in driving customers to purchase and ultimately to advocacy. They spend a huge amount of money to build that early advantage of popularity and subsequently rely on the "natural progression" of customers in their path to purchase, without really making the necessary intervention.

Brand awareness is indeed important, and brand managers realize this. They regularly conduct research to track how well the market actually remembers and recognizes their brands. Spontaneous—and especially top-of-mind—recall is usually their goal. Some even believe that share of top-of-mind recall is a good predictor of market share. This is true in some industries that have low customer engagement and a short purchase cycle (e.g., in consumer packaged goods, where awareness alone sometimes leads to purchase). But in industries with high customer engagement and a long purchase cycle, awareness is only the beginning of the job.

In a separate room across the hall, service managers are tracking customer satisfaction and loyalty. A large number of delighted customers is reflected in a high loyalty index. Loyalty itself has been redefined as customer willingness to recommend a particular brand. Thus, the ultimate goal on this end is to reach a high number of customers who are willing to advocate their brands—that is, a higher brand advocacy than that of other brands.

Metrics such as awareness and advocacy, however, have inherent weaknesses; they focus more on the outcome rather than the process to reach the goal. The metrics are useful for tracking a brand's progress and for measuring the performance of the brand and the service teams. But brand and service managers often face difficulties understanding why their scores go up or down in any given quarter. Consequently, changes in the results are not being followed up with any marketing interventions.

Moreover, brand managers and service managers do not necessarily talk to each other when it comes to conducting and analyzing their own research. Because of these organizational silos, companies often fail to see any correlation between awareness and advocacy. They miss the simple but important insight into how effective they are in converting people who may be aware of their brands in the market into customers and even into loyal advocates.

Introducing PAR and BAR

A new set of metrics should be introduced to solve the problems with the current measurement. In line with the five A's, two metrics are valuable to measure: *purchase action ratio* (PAR) and *brand advocacy ratio* (BAR). PAR measures how well companies "convert" brand awareness into brand purchase. BAR measures how good companies "convert" brand awareness into brand advocacy. Essentially, we are tracking the number of customers who go from *aware* (A1) to *act* (A4) and eventually to *advocate* (A5).

From a population of 100 people in the market, for example, Brand X is spontaneously recalled by 90 people; out of that 90, only 18 people end up buying the brand, and only 9 spontaneously recommend the brand. Therefore, the PAR for Brand X is 18/90 or 0.2 and the BAR is 9/90 or 0.1. On the surface, Brand X looks promising since it has a brand awareness of 0.9, but in fact it performs rather poorly. It fails to convert 80% of the high level of brand awareness into sales. (See Figure 6.1.)

These two simple metrics are patterned after the sort of ratios that finance executives use to measure financial health, such as return on equity (ROE), which measures how much profit a company generates

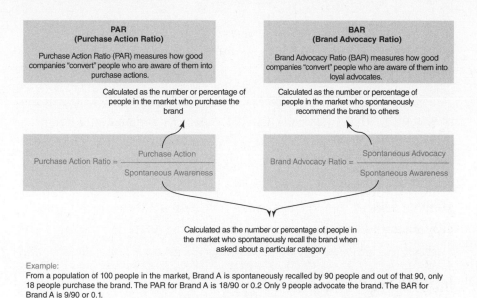

Example:
From a population of 100 people in the market, Brand A is spontaneously recalled by 90 people and out of that 90, only 18 people purchase the brand. The PAR for Brand A is 18/90 or 0.2 Only 9 people advocate the brand. The BAR for Brand A is 9/90 or 0.1.

Figure 6.1 New Productivity Metrics (PAR and BAR)

with the equity shareholders have invested. ROE helps shareholders keep track of the "productivity" of their money. Similarly, PAR and BAR allow marketers to measure the productivity of their spending, particularly for generating brand awareness.

It turns out that PAR and BAR are indeed better measurements for return on marketing investment (ROMI). For most industries, the biggest marketing spending goes to raising awareness through advertising. Thus, we can consider brand awareness a proxy for "marketing investment" in the ROMI equation. The "return," on the other hand, is twofold. The first is *purchase action* which, from a company's perspective, directly translates to sales. The second is *advocacy*, which indirectly translates to sales growth.

Decomposing PAR and BAR

The value of the metrics does not stop there. When companies manage to measure "conversion rate" from awareness to advocacy, they can answer the overriding question: How do companies make necessary interventions and increase the number of loyal advocates?

Again drawing insight from finance executives, we should break PAR and BAR into their elements. In a DuPont analysis, ROE is seen as the product of three major parts: *profitability* (as measured by net profit margin), *asset use efficiency* (as measured by asset turnover), and *financial leverage* (as measured by equity multiplier). When comparing brands, a higher ROE might result from higher profitability, more efficient asset use, and higher leverage. A better ROE due to the first two causes is clearly a great result. But a better ROE due to higher leverage requires a more careful examination to determine whether the company is over-leveraged or under-leveraged.

Breaking down PAR and BAR can reveal similarly useful insights. It turns out that PAR may be calculated by dividing *market share* by *brand awareness.* Accordingly, marketers may roughly estimate the potential market share increase of their brands if they increase the awareness of those brands. (See Figure 6.2.)

For example, Brand X wishes to spend more to increase its brand awareness by 1%. From a previous study, Brand X knows that its PAR score is 0.5. This means that half of Brand X's spending is being

Figure 6.2 Purchase Action Ratio (PAR)

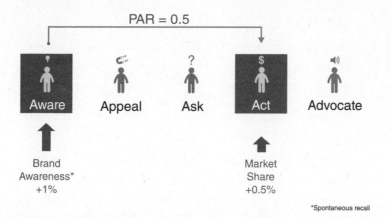

Figure 6.3 What PAR Really Means

wasted in the process of generating market share. All other things being equal, Brand X may expect to have a market share increase of 0.5%. Although this is a ballpark estimate, it helps marketers plan their spending more accountably. (See Figure 6.3.)

Marketers should also measure every conversion rate from awareness to advocacy. A low conversion rate from *aware* to *appeal* for a brand reflects low customer *attraction*. It indicates that customers who are made aware of the brand do not find it appealing. That may stem from poor positioning or poor marketing communications execution. Fixing these problems may result in an *attraction level* of closer to 1.

A low conversion rate from *appeal* to *ask* for a brand is a sign of low customer *curiosity*. Customers do not feel compelled to ask questions and research the brand further. This usually stems from a company's inability to trigger conversation and facilitate information sharing among customers. However, the *curiosity level* of a brand should never be overly high. When customers have too many questions about the brand, it means the brand message is unclear. A curiosity level that is too high also requires the sufficient capacity of brands to answer customer questions directly (through their own communication channels) and indirectly (through loyal advocates). Unfortunately, marketers can never control the outcome of conversations with advocates. Therefore, among conversion rates across the five A's, *curiosity level* is the only one that should not be closer to 1.

A low conversion rate from *ask* to *act* for a brand indicates low *commitment*; people are talking about the brand without making the commitment to buy. Usually this means that the brand has failed to convert confirmed interest into purchase through its distribution channel. There are many possible marketing mix (four P's—product, price, place, promotion) flaws that may contribute to this failure; customers might find the actual product to be disappointing during trial, the price might be too high, the salesperson is not convincing enough, or the product is not readily available in the market. Fixing these issues will help the brand to increase the *commitment level.*

A low conversion rate from *act* to *advocate* for a brand indicates low affinity; customers who have experienced the brand are not delighted enough to recommend it. The low conversion rate may be a result of poor post-sales service or poor product performance. Customers are attracted to buy the brand but are eventually disappointed with their purchase. Improving the usage experience will help increase the *affinity level.* (See Figure 6.4.)

When broken down into their elements, PAR and BAR scores reflect the process rather than just the outcome. Building customer loyalty is a long, spiral process of creating attraction, triggering

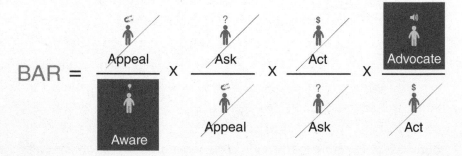

Figure 6.4 What BAR Really Means

curiosity, securing commitment, and finally building affinity. Ideally for a brand, every customer who interacts with the brand goes through the entire five A's unscathed. In other words, the ideal BAR score is 1: every customer who is aware of the brand eventually recommends the brand. But in the real world, a perfect BAR score of 1 rarely occurs. More often, a certain proportion of customers drops out and does not complete the entire five A's.

A lower conversion rate in any given stage across the five A's reveals a bottleneck. Like a bottleneck in manufacturing, a bottleneck in the five A's reduces the productivity of the entire customer path. Identifying the bottleneck that limits PAR and BAR scores allows marketers to pinpoint the problem and fix it. Using this simple diagnostic process, marketers now know exactly what intervention to make across the customer path. Instead of trying to improve across the board, marketers may now focus their attention on what really matters. Altering the right bottleneck touchpoint often leads to higher PAR and BAR scores that are closer to 1. The objective to this entire exercise is to improve marketing productivity and avoid unnecessary waste in marketing spending. (See Figure 6.5.)

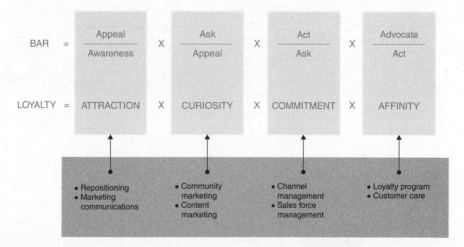

Figure 6.5 Possible Company Intervention to Increase Conversion Rates

Driving Up Productivity

One way of obtaining more loyal advocates is to improve awareness. The more people recall a brand, the more likely it is the brand will be recommended. But this approach is costly, and it has been forcing companies to fight for share of voice with a high marketing communications budget. How should marketers improve brand awareness without increasing the marketing budget significantly?

The biggest benefit of connectivity in the customer path is the opportunity to increase awareness by triggering a conversation among customers. A customer who was not aware of a brand may end up knowing about the brand after listening to a conversation.

We should think about customer conversations as leverage. In finance, debt provides leverage. It creates a multiplying effect without increasing shareholder equity. In good times, debt amplifies profits, whereas in bad times, debt amplifies losses. Leverage helps a company to increase the potential return on its investment. But a company with significantly more debt than shareholder equity is considered to be highly leveraged and carries high risks of default.

In the digital age, customer conversation—or *others'* influence—is equivalent to the "debt," and advertising—or *outer* influence—is equivalent to the "equity." Customer conversation provides leverage. It is essentially a low-cost way to build awareness without relying too much on advertising. But it comes with risks. Customer conversation is notoriously wild; companies cannot directly control the content. When the conversation is favorable, it amplifies the brand's equity. But when it is not, it damages the brand. The favorability of the brand is totally in the hands of customers. Brands with authentic differentiation embedded in their DNA have a better probability of entering into favorable conversations.

Building customer conversations around brands has its benefits. It allows companies to reduce the volume of their advertising and consequently to increase their marketing productivity. But even the best brands in the world cannot rely solely on customer conversations. Every now and then, the brands must run advertising campaigns to avoid the risks of being highly leveraged. They need to influence the direction of the conversation from the outside.

An alternative approach to create more loyal advocates is to improve PAR and BAR scores by improving the critical touchpoints across customer path from awareness to advocacy. To overcome each of the four potential bottlenecks that normally occur across the five A's, marketers need a set of strategies and tactics. Each solution set aims at addressing the underlying problem that keeps customers from moving forward to the next stage.

1: Increase Attraction

If most customers do not find a brand appealing although they are familiar with it, then the brand has an attraction problem. This problem may come from the product that the brand represents or from the brand itself. When the actual product's value propositions are not attractive, even a clever brand campaign and a huge budget may not help. Poor brand communications execution may also cause low attraction, even though the actual value propositions are superior.

So, what makes a brand appealing nowadays? In the digital age where customers are surrounded by technology-based interaction, brands that are humanized become the most appealing. Customers are increasingly looking for human-centric brands—brands whose characters resemble those of humans and are capable of interacting with customers as equal friends.

Some customers are attracted to brands that uphold strong social and environmental values. These brands are practicing Marketing 3.0 and provide feel-good factors for customers. A brand like The Body Shop is delivering sociocultural transformation. It promotes social justice in many ways: empowerment of women, fair trade, and employee diversity. Since the death of the founder Anita Roddick, however, the brand has somewhat lost its "activism" appeal. To revive the brand, on its 40th birthday it launched its "Enrich not Exploit" campaign. It aimed to attract hard-core customers who actively support the brand's mission as well as customers who feel good buying such a socially responsible brand.

Another example is BRI, which actively creates bottom-of-pyramid entrepreneurs to alleviate poverty. As the world's largest micro-lender and also Indonesia's most profitable bank, it pursues this mission seriously. The bank recently acquired and launched its own satellite—the first bank in the world to do so—which enables it to better serve customers all over the country, especially the entrepreneurial poor in remote areas. Timberland is another leading example. The outdoor-lifestyle brand recently pledged to plant 10 million trees (cumulatively, since 2001) and use renewable sources to supply half of its facilities' energy requirements.

Customers may also be attracted to brands that are experiential and represent certain lifestyle movements. These brands have unorthodox ways of doing business and therefore are perceived to be cool. They sway customers with great storytelling about their larger-than-life missions. Casper, a mattress brand, is redefining how people buy mattresses and helping people sleep better. It engages in business practices that are uncommon in the industry. It sells only one "perfect" type of mattress, one designed to give the best quality of sleep, while competitors offer many variants. It sells online and compresses a queen-sized mattress into a shipping friendly 21-by-21-by-42-inch box. Not only that, it provides a 100-night trial, free shipping and returns. It is very convenient and risk-free for customers who do not have time to select the right models and transport the mattress. Casper's ability to remain attractive in the long run, however, remains to be seen.

Tesla is another example of a lifestyle brand that has wide appeal. Customers are waiting in line for a couple of years to get their Tesla. With the Steve Jobs–like persona of Elon Musk, the brand tells appealing stories about the future of cars and the sustainable-energy movement. A brand like Tesla provides customers a platform on which to express themselves. For customers, owning a Tesla is about both having a great driving experience and making a statement of who they are.

Many customers may also be attracted to brands that are able to personalize their products and services to meet customers' exact needs. We are living in a world where demand is fragmented and the market is heterogeneous. In a simple fashion, Burger King started the trend of customization by launching its "Have It Your Way" campaign in the mid-1970s.

Decades later, the trend of customization is still going strong. Fortunately, technology has enabled brands to do mass customization. The brands may use big-data analytics to understand an individual customer's behavior and preference. That way, the brands may provide customers with what they want, when they want it, and where they want it. NIKEiD, which allows customers to design their own shoes and sports apparel, is one of the most successful brands in the area of mass customization.

It is important for a brand to have authentic differentiation that brings strong appeal. The more bold, audacious, and unorthodox the differentiation is, the greater the brand's appeal is.

2: Optimize Curiosity

George Loewenstein of Carnegie Mellon provides one of the simplest definitions of curiosity: the feeling of deprivation that comes from an information gap between what we know and what we want to know.

Separately, physiologists Jean Piaget and Daniel Berlyne found a correlation between surprise and curiosity. Piaget argued that curiosity follows an inverted u–shaped curve; we are most curious when there is an optimum level of deviation between what we expect and what we actually experience. When we have little or no expectation at all, we have no reason to be curious. When we have a strong expectation, we tend to avoid finding out the "truth" and therefore have low curiosity. Berlyne also argued that when people confront surprises, they feel aroused and start to explore further.

In marketing, curiosity comes from providing customers with appealing knowledge without giving too much away. Thus, creating curiosity involves an approach known as *content marketing*: a set of activities of creating and distributing content that is relevant to the lives of customers but also strongly associated with a certain brand.

In some cases, the brand is obvious and is the one driving the traffic toward the contents. Examples of this include General Electric, which provides content that involves science, and Chase, which provides interesting content that focuses on financial planning and lifestyle on its websites.

In other cases, customers often come across certain content that they find interesting while browsing and searching the Internet. Upon exploring the content further, they may discover that a certain brand is the one behind the intriguing content and may ultimately come to appreciate the brand. GE's sci-fi podcast *The Message* and its online magazine *Txchnologist* are examples of this. Another example is *Departures*, a luxury magazine covering travel, fashion, shopping, lifestyle, and art and culture. Upon browsing the website, readers often stumble upon exclusive content available only for American Express customers. *Departures* was eventually acquired from American Express by *Time* Inc. in 2013.

Content ideation and the creation process is one-half of content marketing. It involves identifying unique themes that are both relevant to the customers and connected to the brands. The content may come in various formats—written formats (articles, white papers, case studies, press releases, and even books) as well as graphic formats (infographics, comics, interactive graphics, games, video, and even movies).

Another half of content marketing is distribution and amplification of the content. Like advertisements, content must be placed in the right media. The simplest way to distribute content is through a company's own media channel e.g., corporate websites and social media accounts). If additional budget is available, native advertising through a paid media channel is an alternative. Essentially, native advertising is about distributing content through well-known publishers, in styles that are considered familiar and native by readers. When content is truly authentic, the content may self-distribute virally through word of mouth and social media sharing. We call this an earned media channel. For this purpose, brands may need to actively do community marketing as well as social media marketing.

To capitalize on curiosity, good marketers make content readily available whenever customers look for it. It should be "searchable" and "shareable." Google introduced what it calls the Zero Moment of Truth (ZMOT), a pre-purchase phase in which customers curiously search for and process more information. It precedes the first interaction with a brand or what it calls First Moment of Truth. Research that Google conducted revealed that "searching online" and "talking to friends and family" are the top two sources of ZMOT. It is the role of marketers to ensure that when customers search online or ask their friends and family, their brands show up in a convincing way.

3: Increase Commitment

Attracting and convincing customers are important steps toward creating loyal brand advocates. Still, the job is far from done. Marketers need to make sure that customers end up buying and using their brands. Imagine a customer who heard about a brand on TV and went online to research that brand further. The customer was finally convinced that the brand was the right choice upon reading what the brand stands for. The customer now seeks to buy the brand online but finds out that it is available only in a store in a remote location. The customer may decide that it is not worth the time to go there and buy the brand. In this scenario, the customer path stops abruptly because the brand fails to ensure availability. The customer may also decide to go to the location to buy the brand. When the store experience— physical evidence, sales process, and salespeople—fails to meet the customer's expectations, the customer path stops as well. Thus, the ability to lock in customer commitment depends on channel availability and the ability to deliver superior experience.

Increasing customer commitment involves omnichannel marketing, which provides an integrated online/offline experience for customers regardless of touchpoints. It may include the customer's experience in a physical store, a website, a mobile application, a call center, or another channel. The key is not just to surround customers with many touchpoint options, but to provide a seamless experience as customers jump from one channel to another. It is important to note that customers are, in fact, channel-agnostic. They do not think in terms of channels, but they expect a consistent and seamless experience along their path to purchase.

Since different touchpoints are managed by different people with different budgets and goals within an organization, the biggest obstacle to delivering a seamless experience consists of the organizational silos, which usually lead to channel conflict. Marketers need to break down these silos and put themselves in the customers' shoes. They need to map the customer path using the most complete scenario and to define the role of each channel so as to drive customers into making the commitment to purchase. In this case, channels should be transformed from market specialists (serving specific market segments) and product specialists (selling specific product categories) into activity specialists (playing specific roles across the customer path). Despite being specialists in specific activities, each channel often is allowed to close a sale.

Macy's is a great example of this. A few years ago, Macy's discovered the relationship between its online and brick-and-mortar business. A dollar spent on search engine optimization drove six dollars of in-store purchase. Since then, Macy's has been integrating its offline and online operations. Customers may search a product on their mobile phone and check its availability in nearby stores. Customers are given the choice of buying the product directly through Macy's e-commerce site or buying it at a nearby store.

Macy's has become channel-agnostic and is indifferent as to whether customers purchase products online or offline. Customers have a higher commitment when they are enabled to make purchases in the moment they want to do so. Macy's has combined two silo budgets into one marketing budget and therefore is able to optimize spending with the unified goal of delivering the best customer experience that drives the most sales.

Walgreens is another example. With its ubiquitous store presence across the United States, Walgreens is able to send personalized offers through its mobile app to nearby customers. The timely and relevant offers trigger customers to make commitments and visit nearby stores to make purchases. The mobile app has driven more than 5 million store visits per week, and people who use the app end up spending six times as much as average store-only customers.

4: Increase Affinity

Marketers with a long-term orientation consider closing a sale as the start of a potentially more rewarding relationship. It is also a key moment of truth in building advocacy. For most customers, post-purchase experience, which includes usage and after-sales service, is often about evaluating whether the actual product or service performance is consistent with the pre-purchase claims made by marketers. When the actual experience matches or even exceeds expectations, customers will develop a sense of affinity and become more likely to be loyal advocates. Consequently, marketers may derive customer lifetime and referral value from the customers.

To improve the post-purchase experience, marketers should extend the touchpoints and allow more interactions with customers beyond the regular ones. To the actual product enjoyment and service experience, marketers may add customer-engagement programs.

As brands are humanizing, customer engagement is indeed becoming important. It breaks the barriers between companies and customers and allows them to interact as friends. In the digital age, marketers need to determine the balance between high-touch and high-tech engagement, depending on the characters of their customers. A broad spectrum of alternative interactions are available to choose from, including various types of customer service interfaces, social-media interactions, and gamification.

Ritz-Carlton has a well-known reputation for using a human touch to engage its customers. The hotel chain is known for empowering its staffs to deliver surprising delight to guests. An example is an occasion when a child's stuffed giraffe went missing during a stay at the hotel. The parents was forced to tell their child a white lie, saying that the giraffe was on a holiday. Ritz-Carlton went to great lengths to corroborate the story and sent documented proof of the giraffe's holiday at the hotel.

Online shoe retailer Zappos, for instance, is well known for its engaging call-center operations. A woman who struggled to find shoes for her damaged feet ordered six pairs of shoes from Zappos, known for its free return. The customer decided to keep two pairs and return the others. After an initial friendly phone conversation, a Zappos rep sent flowers to the customer just to let her know that she sympathized with her.

Social media is also a powerful tool for customer engagement. A research by Rilling, Sanfey, Aronson, Nystrom, and Cohen revealed the reason why social media became so popular. Their study shows that for humans, face-to-face interaction demands more emotional involvement than human-to-machine interaction does. Communicating through instant messaging and social media tools has thus become easy for people. When customers want to avoid emotionally demanding interaction—for example, when making a complaint about poor service—they often opt for the electronic interface. A survey by J.D. Power revealed that 67 percent of U.S. customers have used a company's social media for servicing purposes.

Another approach to build engagements that are enjoyable for customers is through *gamification*, which is the use of game mechanics to increase engagement with a brand. Because games are fun, addictive, and competitive, they encourage certain customer behavior subconsciously.

The Starbucks Rewards program is a way for the coffee chain brand to build strong engagement with its customers. It rewards customers for every transaction across different levels and milestones, each with different perks and benefits. The objective is to motivate customers to increase transactions and improve their status.

Walgreens also engages customers through gamification. Integrated with activity trackers, the Walgreens app rewards customers who engage in healthy behaviors, such as walking, running, or cycling. OCBC Bank, in collaboration with PlayMoolah, teaches children to make smart financial decisions with the use of games. With gamification, children are subconsciously taught that every decision they make has implications.

Summary: Purchase Action Ratio and Brand Advocacy Ratio

In line with the five A's customer path, we have introduced a set of new metrics. These are purchase action ratio (PAR) and brand advocacy ratio (BAR), which can better evaluate how effective marketers are in driving customers from *awareness* to *action* and finally to *advocacy*. In essence, PAR and BAR allow marketers to measure the productivity of their marketing activities.

Reflection Questions

- How can your business adopt the new metrics of PAR and BAR to measure marketing productivity?

- How can your business trigger favorable customer conversations in order to drive awareness without increasing the marketing budget significantly?

7 Industry Archetypes and Best Practices

Channel, Brand, Sales, and Service Management

To understand market results, we need to make use of the concept of the customer path. It shows how the customer moves from no awareness of a product or service to high awareness, interest, purchase, repurchase, and even word of mouth.

In real life, customer paths are very complex and heterogeneous and involve diverse traditional and digital media combinations. The market in which the brands play influences the complexity of the customer path. An industry with low purchase risks—typically due to low price points and high purchase frequency—typically has a simpler and shorter customer path. On the other hand, an industry with high purchase risks typically has high customer involvements and therefore a more complex and longer customer path. Moreover, the same industry often exhibits different customer-path patterns in different geographical markets.

Even in the same industry and in the same geographical area, different brands can show different customer-path patterns. Bigger brands tend to have more touchpoints, which allow customers to experience a wider set of interaction possibilities. Smaller brands typically have a deeper intimacy and a limited number of touchpoints. The characteristics of the customer segments that the brands engage with and the brand positioning decisions also contribute to this heterogeneity.

That is why we simplify diverse customer path possibilities into the generic five A's framework, which can be applied to all industries. With the same generic framework, we are able to derive patterns that define several key industry archetypes. Especially in the era of technological convergence and disruptive innovation, the walls between industries are blurring. Using the five A's framework, we can learn how other industries cope with their challenges. Moreover, we can draw insights on how to win in a specific industry by comparing the brand advocacy ratio (BAR) statistics.

Four Major Industry Archetypes

Visualizing conversion rates—attraction, curiosity, commitment, and affinity levels—across the five A's helps uncover important insights into industry characteristics. We found at least four major patterns that exist across industries: "door knob," "goldfish," "trumpet," and "funnel." Each pattern represents a distinct industry archetype, each with a specific customer behavior model and a different set of challenges. (See Figure 7.1.)

Pattern 1: Door Knob

The first major and most common pattern is the door knob. The most distinctive feature of the door knob pattern is the high commitment despite the low curiosity level. A well-known industry with the "door knob" customer path is consumer packaged goods (CPG).

In the door knob pattern, customers do not spend time to research and evaluate options. Since the price points are relatively low,

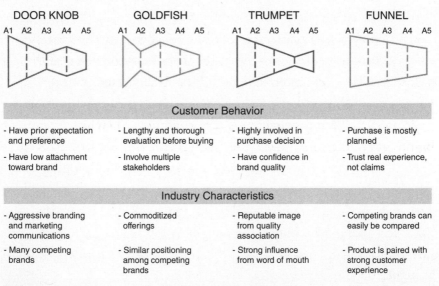

Figure 7.1 Mapping Industry Archetypes

customers do not feel the need to learn more about competing brands. Moreover, purchases are usually frequent and habitual. Thus, customers already have expectations and preferences regarding certain brands from past experience.

A typical door knob category is also highly fragmented with a large number of brands competing for millions of customers. Due to the emotional nature of the purchase decision, many brands in the same categories may occupy a distinctive positioning in customers' minds despite having similar product specifications.

Purchases are often instant and impulsive, driven by relatively low prices and tempting promotions. Hence, competing brands often spend huge amounts of money to sway customers in their direction with appealing marketing communications. This tendency often initiates brand wars among major rivals pursuing higher market share.

Availability at the point of purchase is also often a key deciding factor within a door knob category. Although customers may not be attracted to a brand, they may end up buying the brand simply because it is the only one available at the point of purchase.

Another key characteristic of the door knob pattern is low customer affinity toward brands they use. Many customers who purchase a brand are not willing to recommend that brand. Since customers have low risks due to low price points, and brands heavily promote their products, brand switching is very common. Therefore, many brands attempt to build customer engagement and improve customer loyalty. Coca-Cola, for example, introduced My Coke Rewards, in which members can earn points by purchasing a bottle of Coke and performing several activities such as playing games and conversing through social media. Based on their points, members are classified into bronze, silver, and gold tiers, with additional benefits available at higher tiers.

Pattern 2: Goldfish

The second major pattern is the goldfish. The most distinguishing feature of the goldfish pattern is a high curiosity level (*ask > appeal*). The goldfish customer-path pattern is found mostly in business-to-business (B2B) contexts.

In a goldfish category, customers typically consider many factors before they decide which brand to choose. Customers often feel the need to ask questions, consider advice from third-party sources, and have multiple interactions with competing brands before making their purchase decision. In many cases, competing brands, even the major ones, are trapped in a highly commoditized industry where advertising rarely works—hence the low attraction level. The industry players often have difficulty designing and conveying their differentiation. In the end, competing players typically offer similar bundled solutions. Thus, customers usually spend more time to evaluate alternatives to find the best offering.

The buying process is typically very long, involving numerous stakeholders with different interests. In most cases, buyers manage a complex buying organization, supported by teams that have strong product knowledge and procurement capability. Both sellers and buyers are often very specialized, with a small number of sellers selling to a small number of buyers. Hence, their research and evaluation processes (the *ask* stage) are often very thorough, and the evaluation results of competing brands are typically very similar. In many cases, customer intimacy becomes the deciding factor.

Although very rare, there are instances of the goldfish pattern found in business-to-consumer markets, especially in industries with high involvement—with high price points—but with very commoditized offerings. An example of this is the travel industry. In a particular case of family travel, the buying decision involves a group of stakeholders (parents and children) and a relatively long buying process.

Benefit and cost comparisons are also a major step in the customer path, reflecting the high degree of *ask*.

Pattern 3: Trumpet

The third major pattern is the trumpet pattern, found mostly in lifestyle categories such as luxury cars, luxury watches, and designer handbags. The uniqueness of this pattern lies in its high affinity levels. People who follow the trumpet pattern typically trust the quality of the category brands. Hence, they are willing to advocate brands even if they do not buy and use those brands. In other words, the number of advocates is higher than the number of actual buyers (*advocate > act*).

In a trumpet category, customers are highly involved in purchase decisions. Their evaluation process, however, is relatively easy, because most brands in a trumpet category have already developed strong yet specific reputations for quality. The quality association is typically built over a long period of time through word of mouth. People who are attracted to certain brands usually connect in communities. The presence of customer communities often influences potential buyers to learn more about that quality.

Due to the very high price points involved, there are fans who aspire but cannot afford to buy brands in a trumpet category. They, however, are more than willing to recommend these brands to others. Even when they can afford the brands at a later stage, they might not have access to them. Most brands in a trumpet category are very niched. Since scarcity increases brand appeal for potential buyers, marketers in a trumpet category do not really focus on expanding channel availability.

Although most CPG categories fall into the door knob pattern, over-the-counter (OTC) drugs typically fall into the trumpet pattern. Non-buyers are willing to recommend trusted brands even though they are not currently using those brands. The key difference between a trumpet pattern in lifestyle products and a trumpet pattern in OTC drugs is in the reason why not all advocates actually buy them. In lifestyle categories, it is all a matter of affordability and accessibility. In OTC drugs, on the other hand, some advocates do not buy their own recommended drugs simply because they do not need the drugs at the moment. When they do, they know which ones to buy.

Pattern 4: Funnel

The fourth major pattern is the traditional funnel. In a funnel category, most purchases are well planned and customers are highly involved in the purchase decisions. In fact, this is the only pattern in which customers go through each stage of the customer path on the road to purchase and advocacy. They ask questions about the brands they like and eventually purchase the brands if they like what they hear from the conversation. They advocate only if they have experienced the product themselves. The funnel pattern is found mostly in consumer durables as well as in service industries.

In a funnel category, the overall customer experience really matters because customers do not skip any stage and may drop brands from their consideration sets anywhere across the customer path. The *act* is especially important for customers given that they would like to immerse themselves in the purchase and usage experience. Hence, unlike in a door knob category where positioning can be superficial, in a funnel category, positioning must be deeply rooted in the actual experience. It is important for brands in a funnel category to manage multiple touchpoints such as advertising (*aware* and *appeal*), website and call center (*ask*), sales channel (*act*), as well as post-purchase services (*advocate*).

Although brand switching is infrequent in a funnel category, a diminishing quality of customer experience over time may prompt customers to consider other brands or even trade up to more premium brands. Since customers continuously expect better customer experience over time, a funnel category is perhaps the one most prone to disruptive innovations. As discussed in Chapter 4, most disruptive innovations—especially those related to emerging technology—occur in industries with high customer-experience expectations such as durables and service industries. Thus, brands in a funnel category should focus on both incremental improvements and customer-experience innovations.

Bow Tie: A Fifth Pattern

Each of the four major patterns of customer path has inherent strengths and shortcomings. Combining all the positive strengths of the four major patterns results in an ideal customer-path pattern, which is shaped like a symmetrical bow tie. (See Figure 7.2.)

The bow tie pattern reflects the key traits of a perfect brand. In a bow tie category, everyone who is aware of a brand is willing to recommend the brand because of its stellar reputation. This means that the brand accomplishes a perfect BAR score of 1 (*aware = advocate*). Moreover, the brand appeal is so strong that everyone who is attracted

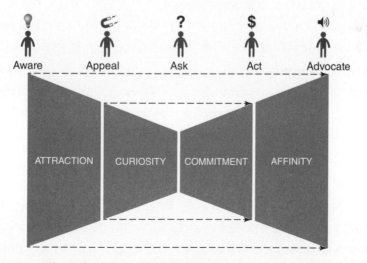

Figure 7.2 The Ideal Bow Tie Pattern

to the brand ends up buying it (*appeal* = *act*). Not everyone who is attracted to the brand feels the need to research further, reflecting a clear positioning and the right level of curiosity. Brands with door knob, goldfish, trumpet, and funnel customer-path patterns should strive to obtain this perfect bow tie pattern.

Superimposing the bow tie on one of the four major patterns reveals gaps and opportunities for improvement. Brands with the door knob customer path may improve their affinity level by building post-purchase engagement programs. This is the challenge faced by many CPG brands amidst overwhelming brand switching. Brands with the trumpet pattern may improve commitment level by improving affordability and channel accessibility without diluting the brand's appeal. Luxury and aspirational brands such as Tesla face such challenges.

Brands with a funnel pattern, on the other hand, should improve both their commitment and affinity levels. This illustrates the significant challenge faced by durables and services brands to balance between sales and after-sales service. But the hardest work needs to be done by brands with the goldfish customer-path pattern. They need not only to improve their commitment and affinity levels but to optimize their curiosity level. Marketers in B2B sectors face this tough challenge because they deal with generally savvy customers. (See Figure 7.3.)

Four Marketing Best Practices

Marketers can also derive industry patterns from BAR statistics. BAR essentially represents a customer's willingness to recommend a brand. In an industry in which the median BAR is low, customers are generally unwilling to recommend competing brands. In this sort of industry, word-of-mouth marketing and social media marketing generally do not work well. When the median BAR is high, on the other hand,

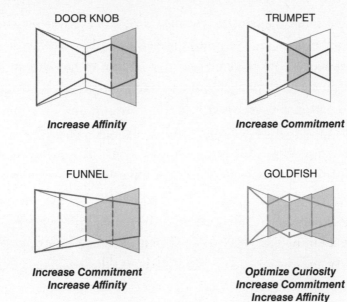

DOOR KNOB

Increase Affinity

TRUMPET

Increase Commitment

FUNNEL

Increase Commitment
Increase Affinity

GOLDFISH

Optimize Curiosity
Increase Commitment
Increase Affinity

Figure 7.3 Improving the Company Path across Industry Archetypes

the likelihood that customers will recommend one or more brands is high. In this case, word-of-mouth marketing and social media marketing are very effective.

The BAR range—the gap between the highest and lowest BAR—in an industry also reveals interesting insights. A wide BAR range reflects a word-of-mouth dominance; there are leading brands with high BAR on top of weaker brands with low BAR. Brands with high BAR have an advantage over others since they already have strong brand reputation that places them on a customer's consideration set. A "pull" marketing approach is highly effective for them. A narrow BAR range, on the other hand, reflects tight competition without BAR dominance. A "push" marketing approach is often the only way to succeed in this situation. It is important to note, however, that market dominance in terms of BAR is not always reflected in the market share dominance, and vice versa.

Using BAR median and BAR range as axes, we may derive another four major industry groupings. In industries with high BAR median and wide BAR range, customers are generally willing to recommend several leading brands. In this group, the key success factor is brand management: developing sound positioning and executing it through marketing communications. Again, CPG categories epitomize this industry group. Marketers may learn the best practices of brand management from leading CPG companies such as P&G and L'Oréal.

In industries with a high BAR median but narrow BAR range, customers are generally willing to recommend certain brands even though there is no player with a dominating BAR score. This group of industries is characterized by either niche local brands or equally strong large players in a highly fragmented market. Success is often determined by channel proximity and accessibility to key markets. Hence, the key success factors are channel management—developing omni-channel presence and driving customers to buy. The typical example of this group is the retail industry. Department stores, specialty stores, and e-commerce sites are known to have strong recommendations from their patrons. Companies such as Macy's and Amazon are leading examples for marketers to learn about driving customers to their sales channels through traditional and digital media.

In industries where the BAR is low but the BAR range is wide, customers do not generally recommend brands, although they sometimes advocate leading brands. Customers typically have poor perceptions of most brands in these industries, despite several exceptions. Customer experience is often polarizing with equal numbers of happy and frustrated customers. Leading brands often show their service excellence and customer intimacy over other brands'. An example of this group is the airline industry. Skytrax's list of the top 10 airlines in the world consists of airlines from the Middle East and Asia such as Qatar Airways and Singapore Airlines that have exceptional service attributes. Their key success factor is service management—managing service processes and service people as well as physical evidence.

The final group of industries has low BAR median and narrow BAR range. In these industries, competition is tight and customers are generally unwilling to recommend competing brands. Since there is almost no effect of word-of-mouth pull in such industries, competing brands have to work hard to push their products and services to the market. Hence, the key success factor is sales-force management— managing productive sales people and driving the right sales activities. (See Figure 7.4.)

The groups are by no means static. With technological convergence and disruptive innovation, the walls between the industry groups are coming down. Marketers need to keep an eye on the shifts in their industries and adapt their strategies accordingly.

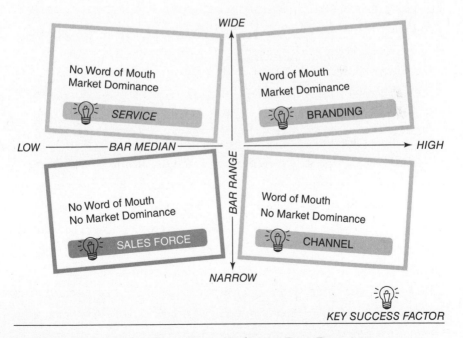

Figure 7.4 Learning from Four Industry Best Practices

Summary: Learning from Different Industries

In analyzing the generic five A's framework and evaluating conversion rates across the different stages, we identify four major patterns for various industries: "door knob," "goldfish," "trumpet," and "funnel." Various industry types can be placed under any of these patterns, each with a specific customer-behavior model and a different set of challenges. We also identify four different industry groups based on BAR statistics, each representing a set of marketing best practices: brand management, channel management, service management, and sales management.

Reflection Questions

- Which archetype best describes your industry? What are some of the key improvement opportunities for your business based on that archetype?

- What is the key success factor in your industry? How can you learn from other industries?

Part III
Tactical Marketing Applications in the Digital Economy

8 Human-Centric Marketing for Brand Attraction

Building Authentic Brands as Friends

In recent marketing literature, customers are almost always portrayed as the most powerful players. Nevertheless, marketers often forget the human side of customers, which is clearly manifest in the digital era; they are not perfect and they feel vulnerable to marketing ploys. Hence they build communities to strengthen their positions.

Marketers need to adapt to this new reality and create brands that behave like humans—approachable and likeable but also vulnerable. Brands should become less intimidating. They should become authentic and honest, admit their flaws, and stop trying to seem perfect. Driven by core values, human-centric brands treat customers as friends, becoming an integral part of their lifestyle.

In Marketing 3.0, we introduced this concept of human-centric marketing as the natural outgrowth of customer-centric marketing (Marketing 2.0) and product-centric marketing (Marketing 1.0). In human-centric marketing, marketers approach customers as whole human beings with minds, hearts, and spirits. Marketers fulfill not only customers' functional and emotional needs but also address their latent anxieties and desires.

As we transition to Marketing 4.0 in an increasingly digital world, we expect a growing importance of human centricity. Marketers need to embrace the power of human-centric marketing even more. Imagine a world where artificial intelligence and robotics are integrated into people's daily lives in the way smartphones were, from automated factories, driverless cars, voice-controlled household bots, to robot doctors and lawyers. Most experts argue it will happen as early as 2025. In such a context, customers will become more anxious than ever as they subconsciously search for their identities, asking "What does it mean to be human in a digital world?"

Human-centric marketing, we believe, is still the key to building brand attraction in the digital era as brands with a human character will arguably be the most differentiated. The process starts by unlocking customers' deepest anxieties and desires. It requires emphatic listening and immersive research into what is known as *digital anthropology*. Once the human side of the customers has been uncovered, it is time for brands to uncover their human side. Brands need to demonstrate human attributes that can attract customers and build human-to-human connections.

Understanding Humans Using Digital Anthropology

Digital anthropology focuses on the nexus between humanity and digital technology. It explores how humans interact with digital interfaces, how they behave in the context of technologies, and how technologies are being used by humans to interact with one another. It can also be used to understand how people perceive brands in their digital communities and what attracts people to certain brands.

The specialty is relatively new in the field of anthropology. But the recent applications in discovering market insights have fueled its popularity among marketers. In the context of human-centric marketing, digital ethnography provides a powerful way to discover the latent human anxieties and desires that brands should address. Several well-known methods that are currently being used by marketers include social listening, netnography, and emphatic research.

Social Listening

Social listening is the proactive process of monitoring what is being said about a brand on the Internet, particularly on social media and online communities. It often involves social media monitoring software to filter massive amounts of unstructured data from social conversations into usable customer intelligence information. Big-data analytics are often used for the purpose of social listening.

Social listening is used in content-marketing evaluation to monitor conversations that happen around distributed content (see Chapter 9). It is also a useful tool for identifying leads and understanding prospects in social selling (see Chapter 10). Social listening is also commonly used in social customer relationship management to identify conversations that contain complaints or negative sentiments and potentially lead to brand crises (see Chapter 11). When marketers track the social conversations around their brands and their competitors' brands, social listening can become an effective tool for competitive intelligence.

Aside from those applications, social listening is most useful for market research. In traditional market research methods (e.g., face-to-face interviews, phone surveys, and online surveys), customers do not always tell marketers what they really think and do. In fact, they are not always able to articulate what they really think and do, even if they want to. Moreover, traditional group-based market research methods (e.g., focus groups) often fail to capture the social dynamics among customers that naturally occur in their real communities. Here is where social listening excels. Customers are more comfortable and open to tell their fellow customers what they think and do. The natural conversations in the customers' own environments help them articulate their deepest anxieties and desires. Social listening truly captures the social dynamics of communities.

Netnography

Developed by Robert Kozinets, netnography (ethnography focused on the internet) is a method that adapts the practice of ethnography to understand human behaviors in e-tribes or online communities. Similar to ethnography, netnography aims to study humans through immersion into their natural communities in an unobtrusive way.

The key difference between netnography and social listening is that netnography often requires the netnographers to become deeply engaged as active participants in online communities. The netnographers join the communities, immerse themselves in the relationships, engage in conversations, and develop empathy toward peer members. Thus, netnography itself is a form of human-to-human connection in the market-research process.

In many cases, netnography becomes a more immersive follow-up of a social listening exercise. Social listening can effectively help netnographers to identity the right communities into which they should immerse themselves. Online communities that become rich sources of insights from netnographers are usually customer-run communities—rather than company-run communities—that cover very specific topics with a sizable traffic and a sizable number of active members. In most cases, it is critical for the netnographers to disclose their purpose in doing the research and ask for permission from the community members.

Whereas social listening mostly uses social media monitoring software to automatically create data visualizations, netnography still requires the researchers to synthesize their deeper insights. Netnography often requires netnographers to reflect on what they observe as well as on what they personally feel as they become members of the communities. Therefore, netnography demands a high level of empathy and a very specific set of skills that not all researchers have.

Emphatic Research

A precursor to human-centered design (HCD), emphatic research is a method—popularized by design companies such as IDEO and frog—that involves the human perspective and empathy in the research process. It typically involves participatory observation and immersion in the context of customer communities with the objective of uncovering latent customer needs. Unlike social listening and netnography, emphatic research requires in-person observation, dialogue, brainstorming, and collaboration among researchers and the community members to synthesize the most relevant insights. Thus, emphatic research is the method closest to traditional ethnography.

To ensure a comprehensive and rich human perspective, the research process typically involves multi-disciplinary team members such as psychologists, anthropologist, product designers, engineers, and marketers. The team members usually go out and immerse themselves into customer communities and observe their frustrations and surprising behaviors. Coming from different backgrounds, each team member typically comes up with different research findings. Thus, the team members need to gather and synthesize their findings with a series of brainstorming sessions. The insights produced this way usually lead to a new product development, a new customer experience, or a new brand campaign that often makes customers delightfully surprised.

The Society of Grownups is an example. The emphatic research conducted by MassMutual and IDEO discovered the latent anxieties and the desires of millennials to become financially literate. MassMutual and IDEO then developed the Society of Grownups, a company that provides financial education specifically for millennials. It provides in-person classes and financial advice sessions in a cool, relaxed, and non-intimidating space that resembles a coffee shop. It also provides stylish digital tools for millennials to use to plan their finances. It ultimately aims to make financial planning an integral part of millennials' social and digital lifestyle.

Building the Six Attributes of Human-Centric Brands

Understanding the human side of customers through digital anthropology studies is the important first step of human-centric marketing.

Equally important is to unveil the human side of brands that can attract customers.

According to Stephen Sampson in his book *Leaders without Titles*, horizontal leaders have six human attributes that attract others to them, even though they have no authority over others: physicality, intellectuality, sociability, emotionality, personability, and morality. These six attributes constitute a complete human being, one who typically becomes a role model. When brands want to influence customers as friends without overpowering them, they must possess these six human attributes.

Physicality

A person who is seen as physically attractive usually has strong influence over others. Thus, brands that aim to have influence over their customers should have physical attractions that make them unique, albeit not perfect.

For brands, physical attractions can come from their brand identities such as well-designed logos or well-crafted taglines. Consider Google and MTV with their dynamic logo systems, which can be flexible instead of static, depending on the context. Google continuously alters its logo to celebrate special moments or persons with its Google Doodle.

Physical attractions can also come from a compelling product design or a solid customer experience design. Consider Apple as an example. Apple is well known to excel not only in its industrial-product design but also in its user-interface design. Apple's user interface is often considered very simple and unintimidating even for non-savvy users. The Apple Store design is also considered one of the best in the retail industry.

Intellectuality

Intellectuality is the human ability to have knowledge, to think, and to generate ideas. Intellectuality is closely related to the ability to think beyond the obvious and the ability to innovate. Brands with strong intellectuality are innovative and have the ability to launch products and services not previously conceived by other players and by the customers. The brands thus demonstrate their ability to effectively solve customers' problems.

When the Tesla automotive company adopted the name of a famous innovator, Nikola Tesla, the brand promised to continuously innovate as did its namesake. The brand does not disappoint; it is in the forefront of major innovations such as electric cars, automotive analytics, and autopilot technologies. The intellectuality of Tesla creates a strong brand appeal, even though it does not advertise.

Major disruptive innovators such as Uber and Airbnb also demonstrate their intellectuality by coming up with services that connect customers and service providers. Major proponents of the so-called sharing economy, Uber and Airbnb are viewed by customers as smart brands.

Sociability

A person with strong sociability is confident in engaging with others, showing good verbal and nonverbal communication skills. Similarly, brands with strong sociability are not afraid of having conversations with their customers. They listen to their customers as well as the conversations among their customers. They answer inquiries and resolve complaints responsively. The brands also engage their customers regularly through multiple communications media. They share interesting content on social media that attracts their customers.

For example, Denny's Diner creates a sociable persona on social media that is friendly, fun, and likeable. The brand regularly posts witty comments and jokes on Twitter that people like and retweet, making it more human. Denny's Diner behaves as a friend to whom people can relate, thereby receiving a lot of word of mouth. Zappos is also known as a very sociable brand. Customers can converse with Zappos's call-center agents for hours discussing shoes and other matters as friends. In fact, Zappos holds the longest customer-service call record at 10 hours and 43 minutes.

Emotionality

People who can connect emotionally with others to drive their actions are very powerful influencers. Brands that evoke emotions can drive favorable customer actions. They connect with customers on an emotional level with inspirational messages. Sometimes, the brands also connect with customers by showing off their humorous side.

Dove is a brand with strong emotionality. A humanized brand, Dove addresses the issue of self-esteem among women by encouraging women to love themselves and appreciate their real beauty. With a massive campaign lasting over a decade, Dove has managed to connect emotionally with women worldwide.

Doritos provides a different example with its SuperBowl 50 "Ultrasound" advertisement, which portrays a pregnant woman who is having an ultrasound while her husband is eating a bag of Doritos. The advertisement ends with the baby shooting out of the womb to get some Doritos. The advertisement turns out to be polarizing; some people consider it hilarious while others see it as disgusting. Nevertheless, a facial tracking technology reveals that the advertisement is the most emotionally engaging, even though the emotions it provokes are mixed.

Personability

People with strong personability have self-awareness; they are conscious of what they are good at while admitting what they still have yet to learn. They show self-confidence and self-motivation to improve themselves. Similarly, brands with strong personability know exactly what they stand for—their raison d'etre. But these brands are also not afraid to show their flaws and take full responsibility for their actions.

Patagonia, for instance, stands for social and environmental sustainability. It aims to minimize the adverse social and environmental impact of its business activities. With its Footprint Chronicles, Patagonia allows customers to trace back the origin of any product that they buy and see the social and environmental footprint of the product. Patagonia is honest and confident enough to show that its business processes are not perfect and still in fact harm the environment. But it is also determined to improve over time.

Domino's is another example. The pizza company made a brave move in 2010 to admit their pizzas were not compelling. In an advertisement, Domino's publicly shared customer feedback about their pizzas. In response, the company reinvented its pizzas and offered them to the critics. The company confidently took responsibility for its flaws, which made the brand more human.

Morality

Morality is about being ethical and having strong integrity. A person with positive moral character has the ability to know the difference between right and wrong. Most important, they have the courage to do the right thing. Similarly, brands with strong morality are values driven. The brands ensure that appropriate ethical considerations become a key part of all business decisions. In fact, some brands put ethical business models as their core differentiation. The brands keep their promises even though customers do not keep track.

Unilever, for instance, announced in 2010 the Unilever Sustainable Living Plan, which aimed to double the size of the business while halving its environmental footprint by 2020. It also aimed to improve the well-being of more than 1 billion people and to enhance the livelihoods of millions of people in the process. The corporate-wide moral compass was translated into brand-level initiatives in a movement to create more humanized brands within the company. Examples include Knorr's effort to fight malnutrition in Nigeria, the effort by Wall's to create micro-entrepreneurs in India, and Omo's campaign to save water in Brazil.

Summary: When Brands Become Humans

More and more, brands are adopting human qualities to attract customers in the human-centric era. This requires unlocking customers' latent anxieties and desires through social listening, netnography, and emphatic research. To effectively address these anxieties and desires, marketers should build the human side of their brands. The brands should be physically attractive, intellectually compelling, socially engaging, and emotionally appealing while at the same time demonstrate strong personability and morality.

Reflection Questions

- What are the deepest anxieties and desires of your customers?
- Does your brand possess human qualities? What can you do to make it more human?

9 Content Marketing for Brand Curiosity

Initiating Conversations with Powerful Storytelling

Content Is the New Ad, #Hashtag Is the New Tagline

In a nutshell, content marketing is a marketing approach that involves creating, curating, distributing, and amplifying content that is interesting, relevant, and useful to a clearly defined audience group in order to create conversations about the content. Content marketing is also considered to be another form of brand journalism and brand publishing that creates deeper connections between brands and customers. Brands that are implementing good content marketing provide customers access to high-quality original content while telling interesting stories about their brands in the process. Content marketing shifts the role of marketers from brand promoters to storytellers.

Today, most corporations have implemented content marketing to a certain extent. A study by the Content Marketing Institute and MarketingProfs revealed that 76 percent of business-to-consumer (B2C) companies and 88 percent of business-to-business (B2B) companies in North America used content marketing in 2016. The B2B companies spent an average of 28 percent of their marketing budget on content marketing, and the B2C companies spent an average of 32 percent. These content marketers would argue that content has become the new advertisement and the #hashtags used in content distribution through social media have equaled the role of traditional taglines.

Content marketing has been a buzzword in a recent years, and it is being touted as the future of advertising in the digital economy. The transparency brought by the internet has indeed given birth to the idea of content marketing. Internet connectivity allows customers to converse and discover the truth about brands. Marketers today face a major hurdle when trying to reach customers with traditional advertising because customers do not always trust it. They prefer to ask friends and family for honest opinions about brands. When they hear claims made by brands, customers clarify the claims by talking to trustworthy peers in their community.

The fact that customers often do not find advertising messages appealing puts additional pressure on marketers. The key role of marketers is to convey the value propositions offered by their brands. Marketers have become very creative in delivering complex information through advertisements without overwhelming the customers, given the limited space and time they can afford in paid media. But the fact is that customers today often find a brand's value propositions irrelevant and dismissible.

Social media has played a major part in this shift. In the past, customers listened attentively to content broadcast by traditional media, including advertising. They simply had no choice. Social media changed all of that. Now, customers have an abundance of user-generated content that they find more credible and, significantly, more appealing than that from traditional media. What makes social media content appealing is that it is voluntary and accessed on demand, which means customers choose to consume the content whenever and wherever they want.

In social media, advertisements cannot significantly interrupt customers while they are consuming content. YouTube TrueView advertisements, for example, can be skipped after five seconds. This has set a precedent that an advertisement is dismissible if the viewer does not like it. We call it "the skippable world's five-second challenge." If brands or advertisers fail to attract attention during the first five seconds, they cannot complain if customers choose to ignore the rest of their content.

This applies also to branded content and sponsored content—the content provided by brands but not in a typical advertising format—on social media. If customers do not find the branded and sponsored content appealing and relevant, they will not spend their time watching it. The fact that the videos that are the most watched and the channels that are the most subscribed to on YouTube are user-generated content and not branded content speaks for itself.

Despite these challenges, marketers recognize the value of social media. Social media, in fact, give marketers the opportunities to leapfrog over traditional media intermediaries and communicate directly to the customers. Unlike traditional media, which rely more on one-to-many broadcasting, social media allow more interactive conversations. These direct two-way conversations with customers are often more effective as well as more cost-efficient. This thinking leads to more brands and companies using content marketing in social media to complement traditional advertising. They aim to ultimately become their own marketing communications media and reduce their dependency on traditional media.

The problem, however, is that marketers often see content marketing as another form of advertising and social media as other forms of broadcast media. Some marketers simply shift their advertisements to social media without significantly reinventing the content. They see content as the longer versions of an advertisement.

We believe a major mindset shift is required. Content is indeed the new advertisement. But the two are totally different. An advertisement contains the information that brands want to convey to help sell their products and services. Content, on the other hand, contains information customers want to use to achieve their own personal and professional objectives.

A 2015 study by Google of thousands of YouTube TrueView advertisements revealed the attributes of videos that viewers do not skip: they contain stories, human faces, and some sorts of animation. It also revealed that including a brand logo in the first 5 seconds of an advertisement increases brand recall, but it also can decrease watch time. Marketers need to realize that their definition of good content might not be the same as the customer's definition. Ultimately, it is the customer's definition that counts.

In order to engage with customers consistently, sometimes marketers need to create content that might not directly contribute to their brand equity or improve their sales numbers but is valuable to customers.

An example of this is Hipmunk's content-marketing strategy. As an online travel company, Hipmunk provides a travel magazine called *Tailwind*, which provides information that customers often look up. A recent article, titled "What Brexit Means for Summer Travel" discusses the impact of the United Kingdom's withdrawal from the European Union on U.S. travelers. Other entries include useful information for travelers such as tipping etiquette around the world and baggage rules for major airlines.

What is more interesting is that Hipmunk also provides an artificial intelligence–powered travel assistant that allows customers to plan their travel without actually doing any research. If customers copy hello@hipmunk.com on an email discussing travel plans, Hipmunk will figure out their travel intentions and will reply to all with a message containing travel recommendations. If customers give Hipmunk permission to view their Google Calendar and the locations of their upcoming trips, it will email them nearby travel recommendations. Considering that the travel industry fits into a "goldfish" category with a typically high degree of *ask* (see Chapter 7), the relevant content that Hipmunk provides actually reduces research efforts by customers and potentially shifts the customer-path pattern one step closer to an ideal "bow tie."

Step-by-Step Content Marketing

In essence, content marketing involves content production and content distribution. An effective content-marketing campaign requires

GOAL SETTING
What do you want to achieve with this content-marketing campaign?
- **Brand-building objective**
- **Sales-growth objective**

AUDIENCE MAPPING
Who are your customers and what are their anxieties and desires?
- **Customer profiling and persona**
- **Customer anxieties and desires**

CONTENT IDEATION & PLANNING
What is the overall content theme and what is the content roadmap?
- **Content theme**
- **Content formats and mix**
- **Content storyline and calendar**

CONTENT CREATION
Who creates the content and when?
- **Content creators: in-house or agencies**
- **Content production schedule**

CONTENT DISTRIBUTION
Where do you want to distribute the content assets?
- **Owned channel**
- **Paid channel**
- **Earned channel**

CONTENT AMPLIFICATION
How do you plan to leverage content assets and interact with customers?
- **Creating conversation around content**
- **Use of buzzers and influencers**

CONTENT-MARKETING EVALUATION
How successful is your content-marketing campaign?
- **Content-marketing metrics**
- **Overall objective achievements**

CONTENT-MARKETING IMPROVEMENT
How do you improve existing content marketing?
- **Content theme change**
- **Content improvement**
- **Content distribution and amplification improvement**

Figure 9.1 Step-by-Step Content Marketing

marketers to create original content in-house or to curate it from external sources. Content marketers should also distribute the content through the best mix of channels. However, the most common pitfall of a content-marketing strategy is to jump right away into content production and distribution without proper pre-production and post-distribution activities. In the following subsections we list the eight major steps of content marketing that marketers should follow. In each step, marketers must check all the right boxes before moving on to the next. (See Figure 9.1.)

Step 1: Goal Setting

Before embarking on a content-marketing journey, marketers should define their goals clearly. Without proper objectives in place, marketers might become lost when they dive deep into content creation and distribution. Their goals should be aligned with their overall business objectives and translated into key metrics, against which the content marketing will be evaluated.

Content-marketing goals can be classified into two major categories. The first category is sales-related goals; these include lead generation, sales closing, cross-sell, up-sell, and sales referral. The second category is brand-related goals; these include brand awareness, brand association, and brand loyalty/advocacy. Most content marketers have more than one objective in both categories. The Content Marketing Institute reveals that the most effective B2C content marketers in North America place importance on brand awareness, loyalty, and engagement as key objectives. On the other hand, B2B content marketers put more emphasis on lead generation and sales as key objectives.

Defining their goals helps marketers to better design a content-marketing strategy. If the objectives fall into the sales-related category, marketers need to make sure that the content distribution channels are well aligned with the sales channels. For example, Birchbox, an online beauty product subscription service, offers tips for maintaining healthier hair in a video. Since one of the goals is sales, a "Shop This Story" pane is placed next to the video pane, allowing audience members to click and buy the products featured in the content directly if they so desire.

On the other hand, if the objectives are more focused on brand metrics, marketers need to make sure that the content is always consistent with the brand's character. An example is Colgate; the "Oral Care Center" content helps build Colgate's brand association as the oral expert. In India, Colgate's Oral Care Center app helps connect dentists to prospective patients, which helps to build a strong brand image in both audience groups.

Step 2: Audience Mapping

Once the objectives have been clearly defined, marketers should determine the audiences they want to focus on. Marketers cannot simply define the audiences in broad terms such as "our customers," "youth in general," or "decision makers." Defining a specific audience subset will help marketers create sharper and deeper content, which in turn contributes to the brand's effective storytelling.

As with traditional segmentation, the audience perimeters can be geographic, demographic, psychographic, and behavioral. The ultimate perimeter is often behavioral. Douglas Holt suggests that content marketers focus on the topics that interest certain subcultures (such as home-schooling, 3-D printing, bird-watching, and body-building) that have the tendency to gather in communities and distribute relevant content among themselves. Since most subcultures are attracted by novel, non-mainstream themes that bind them together, content marketers might find non-generic content ideas when observing them. Moreover, most subculture activists are influencers who will help amplify the content.

After marketers have set their audience boundaries, they need to profile the audiences and describe their personas, which will help them imagine what the audience actually looks like in real life. Through proper research, they also need to discover their anxieties and desires—or pain points and aspirations—which will define their need for specific content. Marketers should then aim to provide content that helps them to relieve their anxieties and achieve their desires.

Airbnb, for instance, focuses on travelers who want to experience their destinations as locals who actually live there, not as tourists. Thus, Airbnb publishes "The Local List" for major destinations. This PDF booklet is a map guide that describes what locals will do and the favorite places they go to in a specific city. It is essentially a travel guide but takes the point of view of a local not of a tourist. The clearly defined audience segment helps Airbnb develop content that is relevant and compelling.

Step 3: Content Ideation and Planning

The next step is to find ideas about what content to create and to perform proper planning. A combination of relevant themes, suitable formats, and solid narratives ensures a successful content-marketing campaign.

In finding the right theme, marketers should consider two things. First, great content has clear relevance to customers' lives. With all the information clutter, content must mean something to the audience to avoid being dismissed. It must relieve their anxieties and help them pursue their desires. Second, effective content has stories that reflect the brand's characters and codes. This means that content must become the bridge that connects the brand's stories to customers' anxieties and desires. Content can be the means for brands to make a difference and leave a legacy—the ultimate goal of Marketing 3.0. This requires marketers to think deeply about their brand mission: what they stand for beyond the value propositions. General Electric (GE), for example, taps into the interests of technology enthusiasts and futurists with its online magazine *Txchnologist*. At the same time, it tries to create futuristic technology stories around the GE brand.

Marketers should also explore the content formats. Content can be presented in written formats: press releases, articles, newsletters, white papers, case studies, and even books. Content can also have a more visual form: infographics, comics, interactive graphics, presentation slides, games, videos, short films, and even feature films. The Content Marketing Institute reported that over 80 percent of B2C companies use illustrations and photos, e-newsletter, videos, and website articles whereas over 80 percent of B2C companies use case studies, blogs, e-newsletters, and in-person events.

Given the trend toward multi-screen content marketing—90 percent of all media interactions today appear on some kind of a screen according to Google—marketers need to consider multiple formats that ensure content visibility and accessibility.

Another element that marketers need to explore at the ideation and planning stage is the overall content-marketing narrative. Content marketing is often episodic, with different small story arcs that support the overall story line. While it is true that content marketing is most effective early in the customer path (especially in building attraction and curiosity at the *appeal* and *ask* stages), the content should be distributed across the entire customer path. The key is often building the right format mix and sequence.

Step 4: Content Creation

All the activities that we have discussed lead to the most important step, which is the content creation itself. Successful content marketers know that content creation is not a part-time job that can be done half-heartedly. Content creation requires enormous commitment in terms of time and budget. If content is not high quality, original, and rich, a content-marketing campaign becomes a waste of time and sometimes backfires.

Some brands choose to create the content themselves. American Express Publishing, for example, managed to publish high-quality editorial content for affluent segments, which include titles such as *Travel + Leisure* and *Food & Wine*. The publishing group was finally sold to *Time* Inc. when banking regulations limited its ability to grow.

Content creation can indeed be a separate business by itself. It demands marketers to act like publishers with strong writers and editors. Good in-house content producers should uphold high standards of journalism and editorial integrity. They should not be biased toward the brand they work for. They should also learn from great Hollywood producers how to create entertaining and compelling stories.

Content creation has no start and end dates. It is a continuous process that requires consistency. Therefore, marketers need to be sure that they have the in-house capability to deliver content over the long term. If they are not so capable, they should consider acquiring the content from external sources. The easiest way is to outsource content creation to professional content producers: journalists, scriptwriters, animators, and videographers.

Another alternative is to sponsor content produced by third-party sources. Consider this surprising fact revealed by the *New York Times*: readers are actually spending roughly the same amount of time on sponsored posts as on news stories. An example of sponsored posts is an article titled "The Surprising Cost of Not Taking a Vacation" by MasterCard that discusses in detail the economic implications of having no vacations. Another possibility is to curate user-generated content. An example of this is Heineken's Ideas Brewery, in which Heineken invited customers to create and share videos and images to redefine how draft beer should be served and drunk in the future.

Step 5: Content Distribution

High-quality content is useless unless it reaches its intended audience. In a sea of content, it is easy for a particular content to get lost in transmission. Marketers need to ensure that their content can be discovered by audiences through proper content distribution. It is true that content marketing was born in the digital era. Contrary to popular belief, however, content marketing is not always performed through digital-media channels. Some content formats and distribution channels are non-digital. Even digital natives use non-digital content marketing. Examples include corporate book publications such as *Delivering Happiness* by Zappos and *The Everything Store* by Amazon. Moreover, B2B and B2C marketers in North America agree that in-person events provide the most effective content-marketing approach, according to a survey by the Content Marketing Institute. In-person events allow the more meaningful human-to-human interactions that digital content marketing lacks.

There are three major categories of media channels that content marketers can use: owned, paid, and earned media. A brand's owned media consist of the channel assets that the brand owns and which are fully under its control. A brand can distribute content to its owned media channels anytime it wants. Owned media include corporate publications, corporate events, websites, blogs, company-managed online communities, email newsletters, social media accounts, mobile phone notifications, and mobile applications that belong to the brand. These are highly targeted media whose reach is typically limited to the brand's existing customers. Even though owned media are free, building and managing them requires significant internal resources.

A brand's paid media, on the other hand, are the channels that the brand pays to distribute its content. They include traditional advertising media such as electronic media, print media, and out-of-home media, along with digital media. In the digital space, the most common paid media channels include display banners, affiliate networks of publishers, search engine listings, paid social media placements, and mobile advertising media. A brand typically pays based on the number of impressions (the number of times the content is shown) or based on the number of actions (the number of times the audience actually follows through with actions such as clicks, registrations, or purchases). Paid media are typically used to reach and acquire new prospective audiences in an effort to build brand awareness and drive traffic to owned media channels.

A brand's earned media include the coverage and exposure gained by the brand due to word of mouth or advocacy. When the quality of the content is very high, the audience often feels compelled to make them viral through social media and communities—hence the organic word of mouth. Earned media exposure can also be a result of a strong public and media relations effort, creating what is known as amplified word of mouth. Earned media typically do not stand alone; they require owned and paid media to generate the free coverage.

Step 6: Content Amplification

The key to a strong earned media distribution is a content amplification strategy. Not all audiences are created equal. When the content reaches key influencers in the intended audience group, that content is more likely to go viral. The first step marketers should do is to identify these influencers. They are respected figures in their communities who have a sizable group of engaged followers and audiences. They are often content creators themselves who have built their reputation over time with great viral content. They are considered experts in their communities.

For these influencers to endorse and spread branded content, the quality of the content is often not sufficient. The rule of reciprocity applies. The key is to build and nurture a win/win relationship with the influencers. Marketers need to make sure that the influencers find it useful for improving their reputations when they spread the content. Some influencers are also keen on expanding their reach, and marketers can help them do that by providing them with access to a larger audience group.

Once the content has been amplified, marketers need to follow through by engaging in conversations. Marketers should listen to the conversations taking place about their content. This can be overwhelming at times considering the magnitude of the conversations and the number of media involved. Thus, marketers must carefully select the conversations in which they want to participate.

Step 7: Content Marketing Evaluation

Evaluation of content marketing success is an important post-distribution step. It involves both the strategic and the tactical performance measurements. Strategically, marketers should evaluate whether the content-marketing strategy achieves the sales-related and the brand-related goals set in Step 1. Since the goals are aligned with the overall business objectives, the evaluation is straightforward and can be integrated with the brand's overall performance measurement.

Tactically, marketers should also evaluate the key content-marketing metrics, which really depend on the choice of formats and media channels. In essence, marketers need to track content performance across the customer path with the help of social listening and analytic tools. There are five categories of metrics that measure whether the content is visible (*aware*), relatable (*appeal*), searchable (*ask*), actionable (*act*), and shareable (*advocate*).

Visibility metrics are about measuring reach and awareness. Most common metrics include impressions (how many times the content is viewed), unique viewers (how many people actually see the content), and brand recall (what percent are able to recall the brand name). Relatability, on the other hand, measures how well the content attracts interest. Metrics include page views per visitor (the number of pages people visit while on a content website), bounce rate (the percentage of people who leave after visiting just one page), and time on site (the duration of the visit), among others. Search metrics typically measure how discoverable content is by using search engines. Important metrics include search-engine positions (content positions on a search engine when looked up through certain keywords) and search engine referrals (how many visits to the company website come from search engine results).

Action metrics are perhaps one of the most important things to track. They essentially measure whether content successfully drives customer to act. Typical metrics include click-through-rate (ratio between the number of clicks and the number of impressions) and other call-to-action conversion rates (percentage of audiences who complete certain actions such as registering and purchasing). Ultimately, marketers need to track how well their content is being shared, which is a proxy for advocacy. Share metrics include share ratio (ratio between the number of shares and the number of impressions) and engagement rate (on Twitter, for example, it is measured by dividing total followers by share actions such as retweets, favorites, replies, and mentions).

Step 8: Content Marketing Improvement

The key advantage of content marketing over traditional marketing is that it is highly accountable; we can track performance by content theme, content format, and distribution channel. Performance tracking is very useful for analyzing and identifying opportunities for improvement at a very granular level. This also means that content marketers can easily experiments with new content themes, formats, and distribution channels.

Since content is very dynamic, periodic improvements of content marketing is essential. Marketers should determine their evaluation and improvement horizons and decide when it is time to change the content-marketing approach. However, it is important to note that content marketing often requires time to have its impact and therefore requires a certain degree of persistence as well consistency in implementation.

Summary: Creating Conversations with Content

More and more marketers are making the shift from advertising to content marketing. A mindset shift is required. Instead of delivering value-proposition messages, marketers should be distributing content that is useful and valuable for the customers. In developing content marketing, marketers often focus on content production and content distribution. However, good content marketing also requires proper pre-production and post-distribution activities. Therefore, there are eight major steps of content marketing that marketers should follow in order to initiate customer conversations.

Reflection Questions

- What is the content that you think will be valuable to your customers?
- How can the content tell a story about your brand?
- How do you plan to execute your content-marketing strategy?

10 Omnichannel Marketing for Brand Commitment

Integrating Traditional and Digital Media and Experiences

The Rise of Omnichannel Marketing

Imagine a scenario in which a customer learns about a product from TV ads. The customer then visits a nearby store to try to experience the product. After examining the product as well as other competing products and consulting with a store attendant, the customer finally decides that the product is the best. The customer then searches for the same product online and buys it there for a better price.

Imagine another scenario in which a customer learns about a product from online banner ads. The customer then searches for more information about the product on social media with a smartphone. A social media post leads the customer to a product comparison website, which the customer quickly browses through. The customer then decides that the product is the best in the market, looks for the nearest store that carries the brand, and finally goes there to buy it.

The former scenario is called "showrooming" and the latter "webrooming." Both are common purchase scenarios in the digital era. Customers have become increasingly mobile and channel-agnostic. They constantly move from one channel to another—from online to offline and vice versa—and expect a seamless and consistent experience without a noticeable disconnect. Unfortunately, traditional marketing channels are not always organized to allow a smooth cross-channel transition. In fact, they are often segregated, having their own sets of goals and strategies. This creates a huge missed opportunity.

The way marketers approach sales and communication channels should change and adapt to this new reality. In the digital era, the customer path is not always straightforward and is sometimes even spiral. Moreover, there are many possible combinations of touchpoints that customers may go through in their path to purchase. Marketers need to guide customers every step of the way through physical and online channels. They also need to be available wherever and whenever customers decide to make a purchase across their path.

Enter *omnichannel marketing*—the practice of integrating multiple channels to create a seamless and consistent customer experience. It requires organizations to break channel silos and unify their goals and strategies. This will ensure a concerted effort across multiple online and offline channels to drive customers into making the commitment to purchase.

Omnichannel marketing has been proven to drive results. A survey by International Data Corporation found that omnichannel buyers typically achieve 30 percent higher lifetime value than single-channel buyers. Macy's even found that its omnichannel buyers were eight times more valuable than its single-channel buyers. Customers have higher commitment when they have options and when they are enabled to purchase an item at the exact moment they want it.

Because of this, leading companies have been implementing omnichannel marketing for years. Macy's—the poster child of omnichannel marketing—has been implementing and improving it since 2008. Brick-and-mortar retailers such as Macy's and Walmart initially saw omnichannel marketing as the response to the growing presence of e-commerce. But they now see integrating their online and offline retail channels as a major growth opportunity. In response, Amazon has also made its foray into the physical world by opening a physical store in Seattle and introducing the Dash Button to automatically order household items. Recent trends show that omnichannel marketing is growing rapidly. In fact, the trends and their technology enablers will propel omnichannel marketing into mainstream practice.

Trend 1: Focusing on Mobile Commerce in the "Now" Economy

As customers become increasingly mobile and connected, time becomes the scarcest resource in their lives. They choose brands that provide the convenience of access and transaction. They expect companies to deliver instant solutions to their needs without the hassles. The speed of delivery is often as important as the products and services themselves. In the "now" economy, real-time marketplaces—the Ubers and the Airbnbs of the world—that connect sellers and buyers are flourishing.

Mobile phones are arguably responsible for this. No other channels beat mobile phones when it comes to proximity to customers. Moreover, no other channels are as personal and convenient as mobile phones. Therefore, when start-ups flood the market with their on-demand services, the adoption level is unprecedented.

As more and more customers make purchases on mobile phones—mobile commerce was 30 percent of the total U.S. e-commerce in 2015 as reported by the Internet Retailer portal—it is imperative for marketers to put mobile devices at the center of their omnichannel strategy.

BMW UK, for instance, now allows customers to buy cars with their mobile phones. When customers scan an image of a BMW car found in print and outdoor advertisements with their mobile phones, they will be taken to the relevant website page to see the car details and complete a purchase. The entire process can take as little as 10 minutes.

The next big category, wearables, can potentially fuel this trend further. Like mobile phones, wearables are almost always in close proximity to customers. In fact, customers are supposed to wear them at all times. Because wearables are attached to the customers, they can also help marketers collect data on customer-path patterns. Since the sales of wearables are projected to exceed 305 million units in 2020 according to Euromonitor, the "now" economy is not showing any signs of slowing down.

Trend 2: Bringing "Webrooming" into Offline Channels

In brick-and-mortar stores, customers often face the daunting task of browsing through a multitude of choices on the shelves and making a purchase decision. Marketers need to assist customers to discover and ultimately purchase their brands amid the clutter and noise within stores.

Sensor technologies (e.g., beacon, near field communication (NFC), and radio frequency identification (RFID)) provide solutions to this problem by bringing "webrooming" into the stores. Retailers (e.g., Apple Store, GameStop, Macy's) can place beacons strategically throughout their stores. The beacons can communicate with customers' smartphones using Bluetooth technology, creating machine-to-machine connections, when they are in close proximity. Thus, beacons allow retailers to track where customers are located inside a store. Moreover, retailers can monitor which departments customers often visit and how much time they spend there. The beacons also trigger retailers to send customized offers to customers' smartphones based on the location. When retailers have richer behavioral data about the customers (e.g., from past purchases), the offers can be very personalized and hence can increase the likelihood of purchase.

Even though customers are interested in highly targeted offers from marketers, they sometimes still feel the need to evaluate the offers. Hence, they search for more information online. When the information "validates" their interest, they will ultimately take the offers. With sensor technologies, retailers are able to facilitate this seamlessly. Burberry, for example, uses sensor technologies in its stores. Clothing items in its stores are equipped with radio frequency identification (RFID) tags, which activate changing room mirrors when customers try them on. On the mirror, customers can watch a video describing the product. Casino, a French supermarket, places near field communication (NFC) tags on its products. When customers tap the tag with their smartphones, they get instant access to product details. Not only that, Casino drives customers all the way to purchase. Customers can scan the tags with their smartphones to add products to their virtual baskets and to check out.

The approach of using machine-to-machine connectivity (the internet of things) brings the simplicity and immediacy of the "webrooming" experience into the offline shopping experience. It allows offline channels to engage customers with relevant digital content that facilitates purchase decisions, such as product details and reviews from peer customers. It significantly enhances the overall omnichannel experience and, more importantly, helps marketers improve sales.

Trend 3: Bringing "Showrooming" into Online Channels

In the digital era, customers can purchase products and services effortlessly and instantly. They can also access a wealth of trustworthy content to facilitate their decision making. But online channels will most likely never completely replace offline channels. Offline shopping is about using the five senses to experience products and services before committing to purchase. Moreover, brick-and-mortar shopping is all about social lifestyle and status; people expect to see and to be seen by other people when they shop offline. It is also about the human-to-human connections that usually happen in offline channels.

To bring the compelling benefits of offline shopping to online channels, marketers can adapt "showrooming" techniques. Tesco in South Korea is a prime example. As one of the busiest peoples in the world with the longest work hours, South Koreans find grocery shopping a major hassle. In response to this, Tesco creates virtual stores—essentially wallpapers resembling grocery store shelves—in public places such as subway stations. Busy customers can shop with their smartphones while waiting for their trains by simply scanning the products they want to buy with the Homeplus app. The products will then be shipped by Tesco and arrive moments after the customers reach home.

IKEA is another example. IKEA realizes that it is challenging for customers to find the furniture that fits their spaces. Thus, with its augmented reality app and printed catalog, IKEA helps customers solve this problem. By placing a printed catalog on the intended location for a piece of furniture and seeing it through the app screen, customers can preview having the furniture in their homes.

This "showrooming" approach allows customers to shop and explore products in physical spaces, utilize their senses, and still have human-to-human connections while shopping. It brings the best of offline experiences to online channels. Moreover, it solves typical challenges associated with online shopping.

Optimizing Omnichannel Experience with Big-Data Analytics

In recent applications, "showrooming" and "webrooming" rely heavily on mobile devices (phones and wearables) as the main interfaces for the customer experience. Beyond their role as interfaces, mobile devices are also effective data-capture tools. Mobile devices serve as the bridge that connects the digital world with the offline world. Marketers are now able to view a seamless picture of customers navigating across online and offline channels, something that was previously not possible. The rich customer data that marketers can potentially capture include customer demographics, customer journey patterns in offline channels, browsing patterns in online channels, social media activities, product and promotion preferences, and transaction records, among others.

Capturing the data is extremely useful for marketers to optimize channel operations. Knowing where customers walk and spend their time inside a store allows marketers to optimize the store layout and visual merchandising. Understanding which promotion works for each individual customer allows marketers to tailor their messages accordingly and avoid sending irrelevant spam. Being able to know exactly where customers are located at any given time makes it possible for marketers to engage them with real-time offers. Moreover, marketers can use collected data for predictive analytics. Tracking historical transaction patterns helps marketers predict what customers will buy next. It ultimately provides the opportunity for marketers to anticipate future customer demands and manage their inventories.

These trends involving mobile commerce, "webrooming," "showrooming," and channel analytics are important for marketers to understand given that they enhance and integrate brands' sales and communication channels to deliver a holistic omnichannel experience.

Step-by-Step Omnichannel Marketing

To develop a good omnichannel marketing strategy, marketers need to view the customer path on a more granular level. Marketers need to map all possible touchpoints and channels across the five A's. Since there are many possible combinations of touchpoints and channels that customers experience, marketers need to identify the most popular ones. The omnichannel marketing strategy should focus on the integration of those most popular channels.

Step 1: Map All Possible Touchpoints and Channels across the Customer Path

The first step in developing an omnichannel marketing strategy is to map all possible touchpoints and channels across the five A's. (See Figure 10.1.) A touchpoint is defined as every direct and indirect customer interaction, online and offline, with a brand and/or other customers in relation to the brand throughout the customer path. It is usually described as an actual action that customers take when they are in each stage of the five A's. For example, in the *aware* stage, customer touchpoints include learning about a product, whereas in the *act* stage,

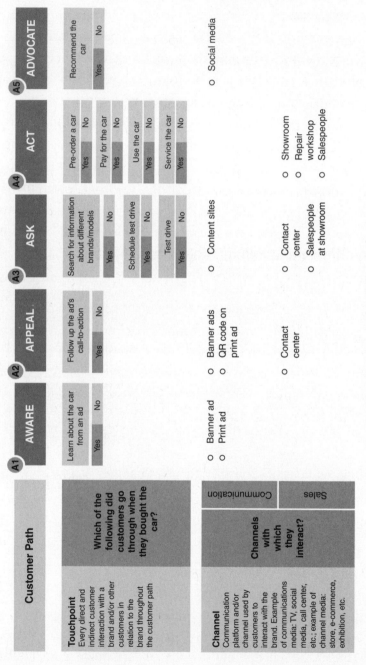

Figure 10.1 Mapping Touchpoints and Channels across the Customer Path

customer touchpoints include purchasing a product, using the product, and servicing it.

A channel, on the other hand, is one of any online and offline intermediaries used by customers to interact with the brand. In general, there are two types of channels: communication and sales channels. Communication channels include any channels that facilitate the transmission of information and content, such as television, print media, social media, content websites, and contact centers, among others. On the other hand, sales channels include any channels that facilitate transactions, such as retail outlets, sales force, e-commerce websites, telesales agents, and sales exhibitions, among others. Sometimes communication and sales channels are closely linked with one another without a clear definition of roles.

A touchpoint might involve one or more channels. For instance, a customer might learn about a product from multiple sources: print ads, online banner ads, contact centers, and salespeople. Similarly, a channel might serve different touchpoints. For example, a contact center might become a channel for customers to learn about a product or become a channel for customers to place an order. These overlapping touchpoint roles and channels are important to ensure that customers undergo a seamless and coherent experience from end to end.

For marketers, more touchpoints and channels lead to more market coverage for their brands. But they also mean more complexity in designing a coherent omnichannel marketing strategy. Marketers need to find the right balance between market coverage and simplicity in planning their omnichannel marketing strategy.

Step 2: Identify the Most Critical Touchpoints and Channels

Any individual customer might choose to experience a different combination of touchpoints across multiple channels in a certain sequence, which we call a customer-path scenario. For instance, a customer buying a car might see an online banner ad, click the ad, and land on a content website where the customer learns more about the car. Furthermore, the customer schedules a test drive and decides to buy after completing it. This is one possible scenario. Another possible scenario is that the customer sees the ad on television, calls the contact center to schedule a test drive, and decides to buy after completing it.

There are many possible scenarios that may add complexity to the omnichannel marketing execution. The focus should be on the most popular ones. Consider the Pareto principle as a rule of thumb: the top 20 percent of all possible scenarios is perhaps being followed by 80 percent of the customers. Company resources should be concentrated on creating a seamless and consistent experience across touchpoints and channels that matter the most. (See Figure 10.2.)

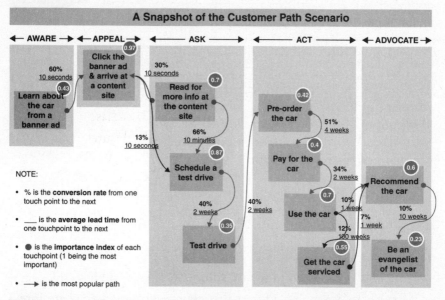

Figure 10.2 Identifying the Most Popular Touchpoints and Channels

Step 3: Improve and Integrate the Most Critical Touchpoints and Channels

The next step is to evaluate and improve the most important channels across the most critical touchpoints, which will determine the success of omnichannel marketing. Companies should also allocate additional financial resources to those important elements.

To deliver a truly omnichannel customer experience, companies should also create an organizational structure that can operationalize the strategy. Companies should break the organizational silos and connect the internal teams responsible for different channels so that they can collaborate to deliver that seamless and consistent experience. In many cases, collaboration works best when companies merge different channel teams, along with their goals and budgets. When they are merged, they will work together seamlessly to figure out the best way to allocate their budgets and achieve their goals, regardless of the channels. The objective becomes unified: to deliver the best customer experience while getting the most sales from omnichannel marketing.

For some organizations that are unable to merge different channel teams, they can cross-incentivize their teams and make sure everyone is motivated to support the omnichannel marketing initiative. For example, contact center agents can be incentivized for their roles in driving customers to purchase, even though the purchase may occur on the e-commerce site. This incentive alignment ensures that everyone within the organization is on board.

Summary: Integrating the Best of Online and Offline Channels

Customers hop from one channel to another and expect a seamless and consistent experience. To address this new reality, marketers are integrating online and offline channels in an attempt to drive customers all the way on their path to purchase. Marketers should aim to combine the best of both worlds—the immediacy of online channels and the intimacy of offline channels. To effectively do this, marketers should focus on the touchpoints and channels that really matter and engage employees in the organization to support the omnichannel marketing strategy.

Reflection Questions

- What are the most important customer touchpoints and channels for your business?
- Have you aligned the channels to support a seamless and consistent experience?

11 Engagement Marketing for Brand Affinity

Harnessing the Power of Mobile Apps, Social CRM, and Gamification

When marketers successfully drive customers from *aware* to *act*, marketers complete what is known as the sales cycle. It is understandable that most marketers put more emphasis on this sales-cycle part of the customer path. However, they should not underestimate the importance of moving customers from *act* to *advocacy*. In fact, this final step in the customer path is what differentiates digital marketing from traditional marketing. In the digital economy, the power of advocacy is amplified by the unprecedented proliferations of mobile connectivity and social media communities.

Converting first-time buyers into loyal advocates involves a series of customer engagement activities. There are essentially three popular techniques that have been proven to increase engagement in the digital era. The first technique involves the use of mobile applications (apps) to enhance the digital customer experience. The next one involves the application of social customer relationship management (CRM) to engage customers in conversations and provide solutions. Ultimately, the use of *gamification* helps improve engagements by driving the right sets of customer behavior. These three methods are not mutually exclusive. In fact, marketers should combine them to arrive at the best outcome.

Enhancing Digital Experiences with Mobile Apps

Consider these facts. More than 70 percent of the global population will own smartphones by 2020, according to the *Ericsson Mobility Report*. Moreover, around 80 percent of mobile data traffic will come from smartphones. What will this smartphone-dominated market entail?

Customers now rely heavily on smartphones to perform several activities. In the United States, most people who own smartphones read news, share content, and learn about communities on their phones, according to the Pew Research Center. In fact, average

Americans check their phones around 46 times a day, according to a study by Deloitte. In the context of after-sales service, a study commissioned by Alcatel-Lucent in Brazil, Japan, the United Kingdom, and the United States found that smartphone users prefer self-service apps to service help desks. People become attached to their smartphones and always keep them close. Smartphones have arguably become the best channels for engaging customers. Therefore, it becomes imperative for marketers to reach out to and engage customers through smartphone apps.

Evidently, most of the top 100 global brands now use mobile apps to engage their customers. These branded apps typically have one or more use cases. First, mobile apps can be launched as media for content (e.g., videos and games). A great example of this is the Pokémon Go app, which uses augmented reality technology. As people go to different places, different Pokémon—some sort of fictional creatures—appears virtually on the app screen, inducing people to travel more and collect their Pokémon.

Second, mobile apps can be launched as self-service channels through which customers access their account information or make transactions. Some examples include the Toyota Financial Services app and the Walgreens app. The Toyota Financial Services app enables Toyota owners to manage their accounts and even make car payments inside the app. The Walgreens app allows customers to refill prescriptions, print photos, and clip coupons, among other things.

Third, mobile apps can be integrated into the core product or service experience. Apps launched by automakers are prime examples. The My BMW Remote app, for example, can be used to unlock or lock a BMW. It can be used to sound the car's horn or flash its lights to make it easy for users to find their vehicles. Audi's MMI Connect app, for instance, has the Picture Destinations feature that allows users to send geo-coded photos from their smartphone to their in-vehicle navigation system. Another example from a different category is the

DirecTV app that allows customers to stream TV shows and set DVRs from anywhere. These apps are synced and integrated into the core product experience.

With mobile apps and their three major use cases, customers can have hassle-free interactions with brands. They now have access to brands in their pockets. At the same time, companies can make cost savings by having the most effective and efficient customer interface.

To develop a good mobile app, marketers must go through several steps. The first thing they must do is to determine the use cases—that is, the objectives that customers aim to achieve by using the app. The next step is to design the key functionalities and the user interface. Finally, marketers need to think about the back-end supports that are required to make the user experience flawless.

Step 1: Determine the Use Cases

Marketers need to conduct proper market research to identify customer frustration points, especially in experiencing their products and services. From those frustration points, marketers should figure out how an app can solve the problems. They need to be able to describe how the app will make customers' lives easier.

For example, L'Oréal found that the biggest hurdle in buying cosmetics online is that customers cannot imagine what the products will look like on them. Therefore, L'Oréal developed an augmented reality app called Makeup Genius that utilizes the smartphone camera as a virtual mirror, thereby allowing customers to experiment with L'Oréal's products. Customers can see what the products will look like on them and share the results on social media.

Step 2: Design the Key Functionalities and User Interface

Once the use cases of the app have been determined, marketers need to design its key functionalities. A major trend in mobile apps is the use of *SoLoMo* (social, location, and mobile). Successful branded apps often have collaboration and sharing features (social), location-based functionalities (location), and on-the-go capabilities (mobile).

A prime example of this is the Nike+ Run Club app, which has all the social, location, and mobile elements. Customers can track their running data (location) and receive coaching on-the-go (mobile). They can also post a running photo along with their running data on social media and compete with friends (social).

The next step is to make sure that the user interface is useable even by people who are not accustomed to using apps. The simplicity of the app is key. It should be so intuitive that users never have to learn how to use it.

Step 3: Develop the Back-End Integration

Most apps cannot stand on their own; they are only the interface that must be integrated with the back-end system. Marketers need to determine how to integrate with the other support elements that customers do not pay attention to but which are critical to their experience.

The integration typically involves the back office, physical outlets, other media channels, and third-party partners. For example, the Walgreens app allows full health services for patients. Patients can refill prescriptions and even have video consultations with doctors. Major efforts were carried out to make sure the customer experience is seamless. Walgreens needed to make sure that the app is connected to the ordering system in their physical outlets. The chain also needed to collaborate with MDLIVE, which offers a network of doctors, to make sure that live doctor consultation works on the mobile app.

Providing Solutions with Social CRM

In recent years, the proliferation of social media has become unstoppable. The Pew Research Center reported that 65 percent of

American adults used social media in 2015, up from only 7 percent in 2005. In 2016 there were 2.3 billion social media users, which represents 31 percent of worldwide population, according to We Are Social.

It has become imperative for brands to connect with customers through social media. Consider this fact reported by the United Kingdom's Internet Advertising Bureau: about 90 percent of customers would actually recommend brands after interacting with them on social media. Similarly, a survey by NM Incite revealed that customers who experience positive social customer care are nearly three times more likely to become advocates. In such context, social CRM—the use of social media to manage brand interactions with the customers and build long-term relationships—will be an essential tool for customer engagement.

Social CRM is a major shift from traditional CRM. Whereas traditional CRM is typically company-driven, social CRM is customer-driven. In traditional CRM, companies dictate the communications with customers using outbound channels that they prefer, such as email and call centers. In social CRM, customers initiate the communications with inbound inquiries through social media. Thus, social CRM knows no business hours and can rarely be automated; customers expect instant and custom responses around the clock.

Due to the nature of social media, social CRM is conversational. Unlike traditional CRM, which is more one-way and cyclical, social CRM involves ongoing dialogues. The dialogues are not only between the brands and the customers but also among customers in their communities. Because of the social dynamics, issues can hardly be contained and isolated. Anyone, including potential customers, can see the brands' responses and jump into the conversation.

There are typically three use cases of social CRM. The first is to listen to the voice of the customer. Brands can extract insights from the general conversations happening on social media regarding them. The second is to involve brands in general conversations. Companies can assign a team to comment and influence conversations in order to obtain more favorable outcomes. The third use case is to handle complaints that potentially lead to brand crises. Companies are expected to provide solutions to customer issues before the issues go viral.

Social CRM is not the same as social media marketing, although the differences between the two techniques are blurring. Social-media marketing involves delivering brand messages and content through social media (see Chapter 9) while social CRM involves resolving customer issues. A good social CRM practice, however, can turn into a good marketing campaign when customers are impressed with the results. Social media marketing is also more dynamic as a result of social media fragmentation. Thus, brands need to be placed in multiple social media platforms to reach more customers and continuously follow the trends of new, emerging platforms. Social CRM is relatively more stable because not many social media platforms are suitable for ongoing dialogues.

In some cases, social media marketing and social CRM coexist. They can either be integrated or segregated, with each option having its own pros and cons. Some brands use separate social media accounts, one for content marketing and another for social CRM. An example of this practice is Nike's social media accounts: @nike.com for the main account (with content marketing) and @nikesupport.com for social CRM. The accountability of managing social media marketing and social CRM within the organization is usually separate, involving different teams and goals. If anything goes wrong in the social CRM, it can be isolated without damaging the main social media account. The weakness of this approach is that the reach is split. The social media marketing account is typically more popular than the social CRM. The communication tonalities of both accounts are also more challenging to unify.

Other brands use one social media account for both purposes. This approach helps to unify the reach and tonality of the brand. However, having a single account does pose a significant risk to the brand. If anything goes wrong in the complaint handling, it will be visible for everyone to see. Seamless, an online food-ordering service, uses a unified Twitter account. Seamless's Twitter account shares a lot of content. It is also known to be very responsive to complaints and inquiries posted on Twitter. Sometimes, however, its social-media sentiments can be overly negative in times of crises—for example, when the ordering system has gone down.

Step 1: Build Sense-and-Respond Capabilities

In social media, the volume of conversations can be overwhelming. Moreover, not all customers directly inquire with brands on social media. Some of them converse only with friends about brands without directly addressing them. Thus, social CRM requires a social listening algorithm to monitor, filter, and prioritize the conversations—distinguishing those that matter from noise. The algorithm should also be designed to identify actionable conversations, cases where brands can jump into the conversation and make a positive impact. It should also be able to scan for major complaints and negative sentiments that usually lead to brand crises. This gives the opportunity for the companies to mitigate the crises before they happen. Companies have many software choices that can help them do this effectively.

Step 2: Develop and Empower Social CRM Agents

As mentioned, social CRM cannot be fully automated. Social media, by nature, are platforms for human-to-human interactions. Thus, a brand that intends to develop a social CRM platform must recruit and develop social CRM agents who can properly represent the brand with a high level of empathy. The agents should have the right personalities and attitudes, reflecting those of the brand. These agents should be trained to converse with customers on behalf of the brand.

Since social-media conversations are heterogeneous, social-caring agents should be empowered with a strong knowledge base. It should contain historical issues and their resolutions as reference points for the agents. Agents should also be encouraged to share their unique stories with one another to enable faster learning. The agents often do not have the answers immediately, because they need to coordinate with other units that are responsible for providing the answers. Therefore, the agents should be properly connected within the system to coordinate with other parties within the organization.

Step 3: Leverage Community Involvement

Companies should realize that in the long run, responding to all the conversations on social media will become an impossible task. A mindset shift is required from traditional one-to-one CRM to social many-to-many CRM. Instead of engaging in the conversations themselves, companies should involve loyal advocates to be volunteers.

Sometimes, letting loyal advocates respond to negative comments really helps the brand. Since peer customers are more credible, they are more likely to be believed. Ultimately, social CRM should be a self-help platform connecting customers within the community. In many established social-CRM communities, they add the element of gamification to reward community contributions. For instance, Cisco developed communities that consist of experts and IT professionals. The communities then become an online support system that can answer questions from fellow members. Contributing members are rewarded with reputation points and badges.

Driving Desired Behavior with Gamification

Gamification—the use of game principles in non-game contexts—is a powerful method to increase customer engagement. It is mostly used in two major contexts of building engagement: loyalty programs and customer communities. Despite a polarization of opinions, the use of gamification has been growing in recent years. A survey by Pew Research Center to over 1,000 technology stakeholders and critics revealed that 53 percent agreed that by 2020 gamification would be mainstream whereas 42 percent argued that it would grow only in certain domains.

The earliest form of gamification for loyalty programs can be seen in the airline industry's frequent-flyer programs, which encourage customers to use the same airline for all their travel needs. Airline customers are offered enrollment in a frequent-flyer program to accumulate points or miles, which can be redeemed for air travel or other products and services. To motivate customers to accumulate points, most programs have customer tiers. The higher tiers, often called elite tiers, are associated with a higher status, which comes with more privileges.

Gamification is also a technique commonly used in online customer communities. TripAdvisor, for example, uses gamification to increase engagement. While in loyalty programs customers are incentivized with reward-redeemable points, in customer communities they are motivated with reputation points, also known as badges. Relying on user-generated content, TripAdvisor needs to make sure of a steady supply of new, high-quality customer reviews.

To do that, TripAdvisor hands out TripCollective badges to reviewers to acknowledge their contributions to the travel community. Reviewers are encouraged to write more reviews to increase their status. There are six tiers from New Reviewer (one review) to Top Contributor (more than 50 reviews). There are also specific badges such as expertise badges (for reviews on a single category such as hotels, restaurants, and attractions) and passport badges (for reviews in at least two destinations). Reviewers are also emailed their ranking in comparison to others and encouraged to write more in order to increase their rankings. These game principles, such as rewarding customers for completing tasks or encouraging competition for higher rankings, have been proven to be highly effective for building continuous engagement.

There are several reasons why gamification is the ultimate tool for engagement. First of all, gamification takes advantage of human desires to achieve higher goals and to be recognized for their achievements. Some customers are motivated by rewards, and some are motivated by self-actualization. As with games, there is also a certain level of addiction involved in pursuing higher tiers. Thus, customers have continuous interactions with the companies, creating stronger affinity.

Moreover, there is a strong accountability in gamification. Rewards are given when customers complete certain transactions, such as buying more products or referring friends. Since privileges are attached to customer tiers, companies give more expensive rewards only to those who truly earn the rewards. Thus, it is useful to estimate the marketing budget; companies can predict exactly how much to spend in order to gain a certain amount of revenue. Points and miles, when tied to redeemable rewards, are forms of virtual currency that are highly accountable as well. For companies, issued points amount to a liability on the balance sheets.

Most importantly, gamification is aligned with converging technologies in the digital economy. Gamification is a smart way to collect customer data, both transactional and non-transactional, that are useful for customization and personalization. Customer tiering itself helps companies to focus on their most important customers. Big-data analytics also allow them to understand customer behavioral patterns that are useful for marketing automation (e.g., in personalized selling, cross-selling, and up-selling).

To use gamification for customer engagement, there are typically three major steps that marketers need to follow. They need to define the objectives in terms of customer actions that they want to trigger with the gamification. Once the objectives have been set, marketers should define how customers can enroll in the gamification program and how they move up and down the tiers. In each customer tier, marketers need to provide certain recognition and reward classes as incentives for customers to move up the tiers.

Step 1: Define Actions to Trigger

There are several actions that a gamification program aims to influence. When customers complete required actions, they earn points. The most common actions that marketers try to influence are transactional actions such as purchases, referrals, and payments. The more customers buy, the more points they receive. In Starbucks Rewards, purchases add up to Star Rewards that customers can redeem for free food and drinks. A gamification program can also trigger customer referrals. Uber, for example, gives away free rides or account credits for customers who invite friends to sign up and ride with Uber. In the case of LendUp—an online lender that gives loans to people with poor credit ratings and who banks normally decline—customers are encouraged to repay their loans on time to earn points.

Marketers can also encourage customers to complete non-transactional tasks. As discussed, a gamification program can also motivate customers to write reviews. Amazon's Top Reviewer Rankings and its Hall of Fame recognize customers who actively write reviews. Customers can also be motivated to provide their personal information. Starbucks Rewards, for example, gives away free drinks on customers' birthdays, thereby incentivizing customers to provide birthday information. Marketers can also reward customers for developing better habits and changing behaviors. LendUp, for example, awards points for borrowers who watch educational videos on how to improve their credit ratings. A start-up called AchieveMint provides points—redeemable for merchandise or cash—for engaging in healthy activities, which it tracks using health apps. A Singapore-based start-up,

Playmoolah, teaches kids how to manage money better with a gamification engine.

Step 2: Define Customer Enrollment and Tiering

Some companies enroll all customers automatically when they collect their first points, which they acquire by making their first purchase, or when customers register and submit personal information. Upon enrolling, customers are encouraged to complete additional tasks to accrue more points, which will contribute to their status. Most companies classify customer status into tiers (e.g., bronze, silver, and gold) to better manage the relationships and costs. Each tier is associated with certain privileges and hence certain costs to serve. With tiering, companies also aim to increase each customer's lifetime value and focus on customers who are the most valuable. Hence, customers feel valued when they receive better services as they achieve a higher status. Since the lifetime value and the costs to serve can be estimated, companies can measure the profitability of each individual customer.

For example, Sephora, a French chain of cosmetic stores, offers a three-tier program. The lowest tier is called Beauty Insider, which allows customers to sign up without making any purchase. Even in the lowest tier, Sephora offers a free birthday gift and free beauty classes. To reach the next two levels—VIB (Very Important Beauty Insider) and VIB Rouge—customers need to spend a certain amount of money on Sephora products.

Customer tiering also allows companies to structurally track the progress of each individual customer in terms of both monetary value and affinity level. In the context of the customer path, customer tiers serve as guideposts as to where customers are along the *act to advocate* spectrum. The higher the tier, the more engaged the customers are and the closer they are to becoming advocates. Tiering, therefore, allows companies to identify their most active and passionate group of customers and to convert them into advocates.

To continuously motivate customers while managing costs, some companies apply a penalty mechanism by which customers can have their tiers downgraded or even reset. The penalty is triggered, for example, when customers become inactive over a given period, miss a certain point requirement threshold, or have expired points. This gaming mechanism is optional for companies, depending on customer characteristics and the program's cost structure.

Step 3: Determine Recognition and Rewards

The next step is to assign certain privileges and rewards that customers are entitled to within the tiers. A good privilege is having exclusive access, which is unavailable without enrollment in the program and is available only for customers in a particular tier. It can be access to better product offers or discounts. LendUp, for example, offers loans with progressively lower rates in higher tiers. It can be access to exclusive products and services, such as Sephora's VIB access to new products. It can also be access to a certain customer interface—for example, a dedicated call-center line or a dedicated customer-service personnel for higher-tier customers.

Another growing trend for rewards is the trend toward instant gratification—rewards that are redeemable right away without waiting for accumulation. Orbitz, for example, allows customers either to redeem their points (called Orbucks) right away for instant cash back or to save them for later. Sometimes instant gratification is rewarded without a tiering system. A classic example of this is McDonald's Happy Meal, which gives away free collectible toys with purchase.

Summary: Mobile Apps, Social CRM, and Gamification

To drive customers from purchase to advocacy, marketers need a series of customer engagement tactics. There are three popular techniques that have been proven to increase engagement in the digital era. First, marketers can use mobile apps to enhance digital customer experience. Second, marketers can use social CRM to engage customers in conversations and provide solutions. Finally, marketers can use gamification to drive the right sets of customer behavior.

Reflection Questions

- How can mobile apps, social CRM, and gamification help you engage your customers?
- What are the challenges of executing customer engagement programs in your business?

EPILOGUE
GETTING TO WOW!

There was once a Texas entrepreneur who was afraid of rejection. Jia Jiang, the entrepreneur, failed a number of times to get funding for his tech start-up. To overcome his worst fear, Jiang decided to draw up a list of 100 absurd requests and face rejections head-on. After a couple of days of rejection therapy success, Jiang went to Krispy Kreme for another therapy session, but his mission fell apart.

Demanded by Jiang to prepare a box of doughnuts with the shape of the Olympic rings, Jackie Braun, a Krispy Kreme worker, did exactly that. Jackie even got the color sequence right. Expecting rejection and ridicule, Jiang instead got a WOW moment. A recording of this (https://www.youtube.com/watch?v=7Ax2CsVbrX0) has been watched over five million times on YouTube. WOW!

What Is a "WOW"?

From Jiang's story, we learn that WOW is an expression that a customer utters when experiencing speechless delight. We also learn that three characteristics constitute a WOW. First, a WOW *is surprising*. When one has a certain expectation but gets much more, that is a WOW moment. A deviation to an expected outcome is what creates a WOW. Second, a WOW *is personal* and can be triggered only by the person experiencing it. If Jiang had not made an odd request, he would have experienced regular service at Krispy Kreme.

A person's hidden anxiety when fulfilled will trigger a WOW moment. Unfortunately, not all customers explicitly say what they desire. Finally, a WOW *is contagious.* One who experiences a WOW moment will advocate and spread the good news to many others. In Jiang's case, Krispy Kreme gained free publicity, reaching 5 million people because of its exceptional service. The WOW factor does not happen every day in our business of serving customers. But when the opportunity arises, it is always worthwhile to take advantage of its viral effect. WOW factors are what ultimately drive customers to advocacy.

From its characteristics, it seems that WOW happens by chance. Can companies and brands create WOW by design? The answer is yes.

In a Marketing 4.0 world where great products and great services are commodities, the WOW factor is what differentiates a brand from its competitors. Companies and brands must never leave the WOW moment to chance. It is possible to design strategy, set up infrastructures and processes, and train people to deliver WOW across the five A's.

Enjoy, Experience, Engage: WOW!

Across customer paths, companies and brands should step up their creativity and improve customer interactions. From the customer's point of view, three levels exists: enjoyment, experience, and engagement.

Those companies and brands that focus on product superiority will simply provide *enjoyment* to their customers. They focus on developing products and services that meet the needs and wants of customers.

But those that push further will deliver compelling customer *experience* on top of products and services. They improve customer interaction with service blueprint and design differentiated between in-store and in-digital experience.

Ultimately, those practicing at the highest level *engage* customers personally and enable them to self-actualize. They design life-transforming personalization on top of the customer experience that addresses individual customer's anxieties and desires.

Are You Ready to WOW?

Winning companies and brands are those that do not leave WOW moments to chance. They create WOW by design. They productively guide customers from *awareness* to *advocacy*. They creatively step up customer interactions from enjoyment to experience to engagement. Are you one of them?

INDEX